MW00986955

The
Tea Party
Movement

Why It Started,
What It's About, and How
You Can Get Involved

Bruce Bexley

TheRationalActor.com

Manufactured in the United States of America

10 9 8 7 6 5 4 3 2 1

ISBN 1442156309
EAN 978-1442156302

To Peaches

Contents

"The evil of the world is made possible by nothing but the sanction you give it."

Ayn Rand, *Atlas Shrugged*

A History of the Tea Party

Americans are defined by their passion for individual liberty. No other nation has fought for the rights of the individual as the early United States did. The Founding Fathers realized how morally unacceptable it was for a distant and exploitative government to meddle in their economic affairs. They understood how fundamentally evil a tax can be, particularly when used against subjects who have no say in the government. They understood it so well that they actually killed to be free of repressive taxes. They went to war, putting the lives of their friends and family in danger and rebelling against their British countrymen for the sake of economic freedom.

Over two centuries later, the spirit of the American Revolution persists. Americans still cherish their individual liberties. They work hard and expect to enjoy the fruits of their labor. They disdain the distant government that punishes their productivity, taxing them more and more with each pay raise. They cringe to see their hard earned dollars siphoned off to Washington to pay the thousands of bureaucrats and politicians who appear terribly busy, yet accomplish terribly little. The political establishment grows in power while they as individuals retain less and less.

Americans have, on a few occasions, struck out to secure their individual liberties. In December, 1773, in what has become the most famous such occasion, American colonists boarded three ships of taxed tea in the Boston Harbor and threw the crates of tea overboard.

The colonists held their "Boston Tea Party" for a variety of reasons. The protest was not merely for lower taxes. The British Parliament had actually just made tea much cheaper for the colonies. It was the principle of having any tax at all. The colonists had no representation in Parliament and therefore rejected Parliament's authority to tax them.

They viewed the Tea Act as one more way for Parliament to control them. The tea tax funded colonial governors and judges, who received their salaries from Parliament, not the colonists, to ensure their dependence on the British government. The act also gave the East India Company a monopoly on tea trade in the colonies, effectively pushing all other competitors out of the market. The colonists feared that if the British government were permitted to take over the tea market, nothing could stop it from taking over other, and possibly more important, markets.

On December 16, 1773, thousands of protesters gathered at Boston's Old South Meeting House led by Samuel Adams. They demanded the ships turn around and take the taxed tea with them. The governor didn't comply. He figured the ragtag team of protesters would eventually give up and submit to the taxes. Little did he know, the American Revolution was brewing beneath his feet. That evening, dozens of men gathered in the harbor and dumped all 342 chests of tea overboard. Their bold move escalated the conflict between the British government and its colonies, ultimately resulting in the birth of a new nation devoted to individual liberty: the United States of America.

To their shame, Americans slowly allowed their freedoms to be diminished over the years. Early Americans never would have agreed to a federal income tax. Today, top earners concede well over one-third of their income to the government. Neither would the country have allowed the enormous spending and "internal improvements" seen today. Such proposals were dismissed as unconstitutional.

The Boston Tea Party was about the American individual claiming the economic freedom that was rightfully his. In February, 2009, a new Tea Party movement was born for the same purpose. The federal government had passed a series of egregious bills in 2008 and 2009: the $700 billion Troubled Asset Relief Program; the $787 billion American Recovery and Reinvestment Act; the $75 billion Homeowners Affordability and Stability Plan; and the $410 billion Omnibus Appropriations Act, among others. The bills were purportedly a response to the economic crisis. The Bush-Obama administrations determined government could fix the crisis by spending as much of the people's wealth as possible, including wealth that hadn't even been created yet. They guaranteed soaring debts as had never been seen before, leading observers to title their plan the "Generational Theft Act."

Liberty-loving Americans were immediately dismayed. Republicans, Democrats, Independents; conservatives, liberals, and libertarians alike; Americans from all sides of the political spectrum spoke out against the government's massive spending and the tax hikes that would inevitably ensue.

On February 16, 2009, the first protest took place in Seattle, Washington under the organization of blogger Liberty Belle.[1] The following day, hundreds of taxpayers rallied in Denver, Colorado as Barack Obama signed the "stimulus" bill.[2] Attendees roasted a pig as a symbol of the pork packed into the legislation. Columnist Michelle Malkin covered the event on her blog, writing "Count us all among the 'chattering classes' appalled at the massive pork and the short-circuited process that paved the way for the trillion-dollar Generational Theft Act."[3] Protesters marched in Mesa, Arizona the next day, and in Overland Park, Kansas shortly after that.

The movement was born. Bloggers quickly spread the word: Americans would not let the big-government, big-spending Republicans and Democrats destroy the country. Rallies were planned for cities across the nation. While a few prominent figures like Malkin lent their support, the movement was essentially grassroots. Individuals were fed up with the government depriving them of their freedom. They decided to take a stand.

The movement was propelled on February 19 when CNBC commentator Rick Santelli ranted against the government bailouts on live television from the floor of the Chicago Board of Trade:

> The government is promoting bad behavior… I'll tell you what, I have an idea. You know, the new administration is big on computers and technology? How 'bout this, president and new administration, why don't you put up a website to have people vote on the internet as a referendum to see if we really want to subsidize the losers' mortgages, or would we like to, at least, buy cars, buy houses in foreclosure, and give them to people that might have a chance to actually prosper down the road, and reward people that could *carry* the water instead of *drink* the water.

> This is America! How many of you people want to pay for your neighbor's mortgage that has an extra bathroom and can't pay their bills? Raise your hand (loud booing). President Obama, are you listening?

The people around Santelli erupted in applause. He announced he would hold a Tea Party in downtown

Chicago in July: "All you capitalists that want to show up at Lake Michigan, I'm going to start organizing!"[4]

Santelli's speech was immediately circulated across the blogosphere, igniting the new Tea Party Movement. Increasing numbers of individuals were motivated to throw Tea Parties of their own. Rush Limbaugh mentioned Santelli's rant on his broadcast:

> ...there is a pulse of revolution starting today. This says so much about the media, too. They could find more of these doubters if they wanted to because they are all over the place. Contrary to what you may have been led to believe, the whole country is not a bunch of lemmings walking over the cliff behind Obama, who can fly. They are not in lockstep with the supreme leader. There's a lot of doubt. There is a lot of anger.[5]

The Obama administration decided to target Santelli in a press conference following his speech. Press Secretary Robert Gibbs stated in his typical, dreary manner that Santelli and his sympathizers clearly had never read the president's spending proposals, otherwise they would support them: "I would encourage him (Santelli) to read the president's plan, and understand that it will help millions of people, many of whom he knows. I'd be more than happy to have him come here and read it. I'd be happy to buy him a cup of coffee. *Decaf.*"[6] The reporters cackled at the joke and moved on. The Obama administration apparently thought disparaging the Tea Party protesters as ignorant kooks would somehow curb the backlash. They were sorely wrong.

A few bloggers had proposed July 4th as a day of nationwide Tea Parties. The date was kept, but many decided July was not soon enough. Hundreds of protests were scheduled for the weekend following Santelli's speech at the initiative of Top Conservatives on Twitter (tcotreport.com) and several other bloggers.[7] On February 27, an estimated 30,000 Americans marched nationwide in over 40 cities.[8] The rally points included Chicago, San Diego, Atlanta, Omaha, Tampa, and Washington, D.C. Over 1,000 protesters gathered at the St. Louis Arch despite brutal, 35-degree weather. Organizer Bill Hennessy said "We'll do this every chance we get until Congress repeals the pork – or we retire them from public life."[9]

Leslie Alexander of the Lafayette, Louisiana Tea Party told reporters, "This is about concerned Americans who would like to take action... We are spending our way into oblivion, and it's apparent to me that our politicians are not listening."[10] Radio show host Jerry Bader spoke at the Green Bay, Wisconsin protest, revving up the crowd with comments like:

> Conservatism is based on I'll take care of me, you take care of you. ... This is often translated to mean we're not compassionate — nothing could be further from the truth... Picking my pocket and deciding what's compassion, is not compassion. When you are forced to be compassionate at the barrel of a gun, we have a word for that, it's *robbery*.[11]

With the February rallies a smashing success, organizers turned their sights to the next big date: Tax Day, April 15, 2009. In the meantime, Tea Parties were held in Salt Lake City; Oklahoma City and Tulsa; Harrisburg, Pennsylvania; Columbia, Missouri; Monroe, Washington; Raleigh, North Carolina; Lexington, Kentucky; Ridgefield, Connecticut; Orlando and Cape Coral, Florida.

Over 5,000 people turned out for a March 15 Tea Party in Cincinnati, Ohio. An attendee told reporters, "I'm frustrated with the way things are going in Congress. They need to remember that they work for us, and right now, we don't approve."[12]

TaxDayTeaParty.com was launched to prepare for the April 15, nationwide rallies. The site declared "REVOLUTION IS BREWING at a city near you!" It defined the parties as "a national collaborative grassroots effort organized by Smart Girl Politics, Top Conservatives on Twitter, the DontGo Movement and many other online groups/coalitions," to protest the "flawed 'Stimulus Bill' and pork filled budget."[13]

The Tax Day Tea Parties exceeded expectations. 750,000 people turned out in over 800 cities.[14] All 50 states had Tea Parties. The crowds were diverse in every regard, the only common denominator being dissatisfaction with the direction of the country. Fox News sent their primetime hosts to Tea Parties across the country and achieved historic ratings. An astounding 4 million people watched Bill O'Reilly's Tea Party coverage on the cable network. Host Glenn Beck boosted his ratings to 2.7 million at the far less prominent 5 pm EST time slot.[15] Beck proclaimed, "Barack Obama is president, not king, and we're still the ones calling the shots."[16]

The Tax Day Tea Parties had barely ended when protesters began gearing up for the Independence Day Tea Parties. Dozens of July 4th rallies were immediately listed on the website ReTeaParty.com. Organizers promised many more Tea Parties to come. Their impact on politicians is yet to be seen, but they at least can be proud to have the whole country asking: Who are these people, and what do they have to say?

Why They
"Tea Party Like It's 1773"

The Tea Parties are baffling to the mainstream media. Why would someone hold a Tea Party? What's so bad about the government spending money? Shouldn't the spending plan be given a chance?

First, the spending plan *has* been given a chance – many times, repeatedly, throughout history. A basic knowledge of history and economics is all one needs to conclude the spending plans will not work.

Government does not create wealth. It obtains its money from taxpayers. To spend money, government must take money from somewhere else. The spending plans proposed by the Bush-Obama administrations do not add any value to the economy – they only move money from one place to another. Republican Herbert Hoover and Democrat Franklin D. Roosevelt spent massive amounts of money to "fix" the economy in the 1930s and 40s. They imposed countless laws, regulations, taxes, oversight committees, government-business partnerships – all a tremendous burden on the day-to-day operations of businesses which otherwise would have been profitable. The consequence of their actions was the Great Depression.

In January, 2009, Barack Obama asserted: "There is no disagreement that we need action by our government, a recovery plan that will help to jumpstart the economy." Actually, the disagreement was immense. The CATO Institute issued a response to Obama's statement signed by over two hundred economists:

> With all due respect Mr. President, that is not true. Notwithstanding reports that all economists are now Keynesians and that we all support a big increase in the burden of government, we the undersigned do not believe that more government spending is a way to improve economic performance. More government spending by Hoover and Roosevelt did not pull the United States economy out of the Great Depression in the 1930s. More government spending did not solve Japan's 'lost decade' in the 1990s. As such, it is a triumph of hope over experience to believe that more government spending

will help the U.S. today. To improve the economy, policymakers should focus on reforms that remove impediments to work, saving, investment and production. Lower tax rates and a reduction in the burden of government are the best ways of using fiscal policy to boost growth.[17]

Obama and Bush weren't the only liars. The majority of politicians across the U.S. and Europe claimed their only option was expansion. They identified the "free market" as the source of their countries' financial woes when, in fact, the ills of the economy could easily be traced back to their meddling. And why not blame the free market? They certainly could not accept blame themselves, thus ending their political careers. By blaming the free market, they diverted attention away from their failures and convinced people to surrender even more control to them.

The government could have reacted to the financial downturn in very different ways. It could have done nothing. Or, even better, it could have scaled back its involvement in the economy. New Zealand responded to the crisis by announcing tax cuts for the country's top earners. Apparently their economists missed the memo that there was "no disagreement" on how government should respond.

The United States once championed the free market. When the 2008 crisis hit, American politicians offered zero free market solutions. They could have cut the bloated budgets by trillions of dollars. They could have lowered taxes on top income earners, the few who could actually "stimulate" the economy with their spending. They could have resolved never to collude with or accept funding from the Democrats who ran Wall Street again. They could have apologized for the outrageous deficit-spending committed by Republicans under George Bush and pledged never to repeat such irresponsibility. Instead they hopped back in bed with Wall Street, attacked top income earners, and spent money like there was no tomorrow.

Imagine if government had responded by scaling back. The economy would already have been well on its way to recovery in early 2009. Investors would have nothing to fear from the government. They would no longer see higher taxes and inflation on the horizon. Entrepreneurs would have incentive to compete. An aspiring car manufacturer wouldn't have to worry about the government propping up failed union-troughs like GM, Ford, and Chrysler. He could be confident in society valuing his superior product over his competitors' lifelong political connections and freezers full of cash. Private citizens would get to keep more of their paychecks to buy new products and invest back in the economy. With every individual empowered to choose which products he wished to purchase, the most desirable outcomes would automatically be reached through invisible market forces. People would still lose their jobs and companies would still fail, but then new jobs and companies would constantly be created.

Change is inevitable. The government can do nothing to stop it. Nor should it want to; the continual changes of a free market system lead to dynamic growth and innovation. By holding people where they are – halting foreclosures, forgiving bad debts, taking over banks and car companies – the government only delays inevitable changes in the economy. Costs must be accounted for, and if the government forgives the debts of Wall Street bankers, every member of society incurs those costs through taxes, inflation, and price instability.

The question is who should pay for a person's failure: the person who failed or his neighbor? Who should pay for a company's failure: the failed company or its competitors? The only just option is the first. If a person or company fails, that person or company should pay for it. What right does government have to force anyone else to pay for it? And if it does shift the cost, what are the long term consequences of that action? Those who failed are rewarded. They have incentive to take even greater risks than before – after all, if things don't work out, Uncle Sam is happy to dole out their competitors' money. Those who succeed are punished. Their increased income brings increased taxes. Their profits are confiscated by the government and used to prop up the worst of their competitors: those who offered an inferior product, operated inefficiently, and took irresponsible risks. What would happen to such a society? The Tea Party protesters know. They see the answer clearly and are terrified by its implications.

Some Tea Party detractors ask why the protesters waited until 2009 to make a fuss, particularly when George Bush was such a big spender. George Bush was, tragically, a profligate spender, but the transgressions of his first 7 years were nothing compared to the colossal spending he issued right before he left office – when, he happily admitted, he had "abandoned free market principles to save the free market system."[18]

$100 billion used to be a huge amount of money. Anti-Iraq War protesters decried the $600 billion battle as unmanageably expensive. Then the Democratic Congress passed President Bush's sweeping, $700 billion bailout, followed by Barack Obama's $1 trillion spending bills. Suddenly a trillion dollars is pocket change for politicians. This dramatic change in spending did not occur until late 2008 at the end of Bush's presidency.

The legislation is monumental. Nothing like it has ever been done in U.S. history. Not only is the dollar amount huge, but the legislation grants the executive branch far more power than George Bush ever tried to claim under the guise of "national security." The text of the first bailout bill dictated that "[decisions] by the Secretary pursuant to the authority of this Act are **non-reviewable** and committed to agency discretion, and **may not be reviewed by any court of law or any administrative agency**."[19] Their decisions may not be reviewed? They've been granted more money than was spent on the Iraq War, and there is to be no check on their power? The legislation is patently unconstitutional: Congress cannot sign over such tremendous power to the executive branch.[20]

The nation that fought and killed to be free of a king and his taxes is once again a nation of kings. The people are subjected to taxation without representation. Elected legislators have no say over the administration of the bailouts, nor does any court or agency. Congress signed over its power to George W. Bush in the fall of 2008. When Barack Obama came to office, he did not relinquish the powers claimed during the financial and national security crises – he only increased them. Now, more than ever, is the time for liberty-loving Americans to be alarmed.[21]

The protesters cite a variety of reasons for their Tea Parties. Some are opposed to the government's massive influx in spending. Others are primarily concerned with the tax increases necessary for Obama's plans. They identify their protests as T.E.A. Parties (Taxed Enough Already). Still others are worried about the general growth in government, or the loss of American entrepreneurship and innovation, or the recent funding of failed organizations like AIG and GM. In the protesters' own words:

"My husband and I were feeling frustrated that the stimulus had passed with very little debate and no one had read it. I said, 'We need to do something'" (Amanda Grosserode, organizer of February 21 Tea Party in Overland Park, Kansas).[22]

"We're going to demonstrate our distrust for the government overspending . . . and the policies they are forcing upon us" (Mark Frimmel, organizer of February 27 Tea Party in Fort Worth, Texas).[23]

"My concern is that this country is going down a dangerous path toward socialism and that's not what my forefathers, or my ancestors, fought and died for" (Allen LaBerteaux, February 27 Tea Party in Atlanta, Georgia).[24]

"We wanted to let the people in Washington know how angry we are about the stimulus bill" (John Hendricks, February 27 Tea Party in Tampa, Florida).[25]

"We've got to stop relying on the federal government… It's not going to get better anytime soon. What they're doing is going to make things worse" (Blayne Sukut, Idahoans for Liberty, February 28 Tea Party in Boise, Idaho).[26]

"The federal government has a taxing and spending addiction. If it's not arrested, it's going to bankrupt the country… This is about concerned Americans who would like to take action. We are spending our way into oblivion, and it's apparent to me that our politicians are not listening" (Leslie Alexander, organizer of March 7 Tea Party in Lafayette, Louisiana).[27]

"We are not spending our own money. We are taxing our children. Our children have no representation and we are taxing their dreams… Common sense tells us that if you find yourself in a hole you stop digging. We are here to say to Mr. Obama, 'Put down that shovel!'" (David Kirkham, organizer of March 6 Tea Party in Salt Lake City, Utah).[28]

"Everybody is digging into our pockets deeper and deeper. We are rushing headlong into socialism and it's just wrong. It's not what this country was founded on" (Greg Zenger, March 6 Tea Party in Salt Lake City, Utah).[29]

"Our Congress has been nonresponsive to the people. We've been issuing correspondence to the Congress running hundreds-to-one against the ways they've been spending and their socialist takeover and they're nonresponsive. This is the next step" (Mary Rehberg, March 7 Tea Party in Green Bay, Wisconsin).[30]

"These are people who believe in limited federal and state government, but who think government has overstepped its limited role in our lives" (Matthew Brouillette, March 7 Tea Party in Pittsburgh, Pennsylvania).[31]

"The attendees generally worry that [the spending] bills are too large, too unfocused, and, in the case of the stimulus bill, too hurriedly passed by Congress. We gathered precisely because we fear what our government is doing and has done. We worry about all of the wasteful spending - by the Obama administration, Congress and, yes, the Bush administration... We believe that the United States, Congress, the president and misguided editorials are leading this nation into a morass of stagnation, stultifying taxation and, eventually, rampant inflation. At the same time, Mr. Obama and others are working to destroy the incentive to earn by punishing the most productive people in our economy. Moreover, Mr. Obama proposes discouraging charitable giving by capping the deductibility of such donations... At our next Tea Party on April 15, we will protest that our taxes are too high because our elected officials pass so much wasteful 'pork' in their legislation" (Bill Hennessy, editorial in the *St. Louis Post-Dispatch* explaining the February 27 Tea Party in St. Louis, Missouri).[32]

"The goal was to get people united, to let people know that they aren't alone in their feelings of despair. We want to speak out against the push toward socialization that we feel is taking place in our country" (Lisa Feroli, co-organizer of March 21 Tea Party in Orlando, Florida).[33]

"We're really scared about what's happening in our country," (Debby Whisenand, March 21 Tea Party in Orlando, Florida).[34]

"These packages are being pushed through with no deliberation. The pork, the earmarks – It just feels out of control… The goal, first and foremost, is to raise awareness and put our politicians of all stripes on notice that we've got an intelligent population who's frightened, frustrated and angry about what's going on. And not just conservatives – all people who value our Constitution" (Pam Fowler, Connecticut Tea Party coordinator).[35]

"We're trying to make people realize it's really up to us to change America. It's time for normal citizens to say enough is enough" (Richard Caster, organizer of April 15 Ozark Tea Party in Mountain Home, Arkansas).[36]

"If we don't change, our kids won't enjoy the same America, the same prosperity… We're not singling any individual or party out, but if we do not stand now, we face a more socialist form of government and loss of freedom" (Emery McClendon, April 18 Tea Party in Fort Wayne, Indiana).[37]

Doug Powers, an attendee of the Lansing, Michigan Tea Parties, wrote a blog post describing his motivation:

For me, these tea parties are about putting an end to waste. Not the waste of money (though obviously that's a major concern), but rather the tragic waste of American ingenuity, innovation, creativity and philanthropy.

Think about the monumental efforts in both time and intellect that are wasted in order to satisfy insane government demands.

I attend the tea parties as a way of showing that it saddens me to know that people who might have otherwise cured a horrible disease, designed grand buildings, created art

and music, invented a car that runs on
kumquats that people actually want to buy,
expanded their businesses, explored the
farthest reaches of the universe or had more
time to devote to charity are now spending
most of their energy trying to figure out a
way to write off their lawnmowers as
dependents.

It's a waste, and it's an insult to those who
helped build this great nation, and to those
who have died defending it. That's why I go
to the tea parties.[38]

On the question of why anti-spending
protests are occurring now under Barack Obama but
were missing under George W. Bush, Erika Franzi
of Jane Q. Republican[39] writes:

Perhaps no legislation has ever been more
aptly named than the 'stimulus.' It remains to
be seen if it will have a stimulating effect on
our economy, but it has already had a
stimulating effect on the consciousness of our
nation. The commitment of our Federal
Government to spend $1 Trillion in taxpayer's

money on projects and programs that are beyond our control pushed us to action. I am the first to admit that we were asleep at our post over the last 2 decades while the Federal Government was growing with increasing speed. We are awake now and we can thank President Obama, Nancy Pelosi, and Harry Reid for providing the $1 trillion alarm.

In any case, we don't have the luxury of looking back and mourning the day that we should have acted. We have to begin today because tomorrow is the day my children ask, 'How did you let this happen?'[40]

Several liberal groups interpreted the Tea Parties as attacks against Barack Obama, even though protesters had been vociferously opposed to the bailouts since they began under George W. Bush. Michelle Malkin explains on her site, "This is every bit as much about Obama as it is about the GOP lemmings who voted for endless bailouts, who demonized their fiscal conservative colleagues who had their heads on straight, and who continue to sponsor and vote for massive government expansions like the $6 billion national service boondoggle."[41] Still, Obama will inevitably be called out during the Tea Parties for the simple reason that he is now the head of the federal government. Moreover, he shows no indication of slowing his massive, deficit spending, nor of taking any responsibility for the debts he is forcing upon the nation. As Jim Treacher says, "When it comes to deficit spending, Obama burns down your house and reminds you that Bush once lit a match."[42]

In sum, the Tea Party movement is a grassroots, nonpartisan effort by individuals who are dismayed by the growth of government under the Bush-Obama administrations. They are not followers of any particular group, party or personality. They genuinely love their country and fear the ways it is being perverted by the present leadership of Republicans and Democrats. Their objective is to make their voices heard. If the Obama administration responds to their requests, their work will have been more worthwhile than expected. If the Obama administration continues to scoff at the Tea Parties, as is most likely, the protesters can at least tell their grandchildren that in 2009, when Western civilization faltered, they spoke against the reckless behavior of their rulers. They did not rely on "hope" alone. They did not abdicate their responsibility to think. They did what they could to secure freedom and prosperity for themselves and for those who came after them.

After the Tea Party

The Left reacted to the Tea Parties with predictable disgust: They want less spending? Lower taxes? People should keep *more* of their money to spend as *they* see fit? Preposterous!

One can be certain of the Tea Parties' effectiveness based on the Left's continual denial of their success. Naysayers scoffed at the Tea Parties as insignificant, totally meaningless, not in the least bit worth observing. Liberal activist David B. Livingstone of Detroit wrote, "Apart from a possible invasion by a half-dozen lightly armed Pillsbury Doughboys, there would seem to be few forces less menacing, or less worthy of being taken seriously, than odd, meandering herds of brain-damaged, tub-gutted, SUV-driving suburban garbage flailing tea bags around and ranting about a new American revolution." For all his carping that the Tea Parties were an irrelevant, fringe movement, Livingstone was oddly distraught. He fumed wildly about the "sad and pathetic" Tea Partiers, calling them "miserable, spoiled suburban babies" and "scum" who needed to either leave the country or be involuntarily subjected to lobotomies.[43]

Newsweek's Howard Fineman predicted the rallies would dwindle to irrelevance before the nationwide, July 4th Tea Parties.[44] Keith Olbermann dismissed the Tea Parties as poorly attended.[45] Rachel Maddow said the "numbers of teabaggers were not particularly large."[46] Nearly one million people in over 800 cities isn't "particularly large"? At what point is a group large enough to matter? Saddam Hussein killed a measly 100,000 Kurds in Iraq. Should that have bothered us onlookers, or was the Kurdish minority too small? Maddow also showed her audience a map of where the rallies had occurred. It indicated Tea Parties were thrown in a whopping five cities. In her defense, it would have been impossible to show all 800 cities marked on one map.

CNN and MSNBC distracted their viewers from the Tea Parties by cracking jokes about "teabagging," an obscure sex act popular among homosexual men and "straight" frat boys.[47] Jejune liberals thought it clever to replace the term Tea Party with "teabagging". They repeatedly referred to Tea Party attendees as "teabaggers" (and snickered every time). CNN host Anderson Cooper

joked, "It's hard to talk when you're teabagging."[48]
Keith Olbermann's *Countdown* on Tax Day devolved
to awkward smut as he told sex joke after sex joke
and tittered at phallic images.[49] Fellow MSNBC
hosts David Shuster and Rachel Maddow
cumulatively spent hours sneering at the
"teabaggers." Needless to say, the repeated
"teabagging" references sunk the debate to an
irretrievable low. Liberty-loving Americans were
trying to discuss economic policy. The liberal
response was to giggle at sex. Their joke was
pathetic not only because of its puerility, but
because no one involved in the Tea Parties even
used the term "teabagging." As Ann Coulter put it,
"You know what else would be hilarious? It would
be hilarious if Hillary Clinton's name were 'Ima
Douche.' Unfortunately, it's not. It was just a dream.
Most people would wake up, realize it was just a
dream and scrap the joke. Not MSNBC hosts."[50]

Elected officials were similarly demeaning,
but not quite as colorful in their language. House
Speaker Nancy Pelosi claimed the Tea Partiers were
being manipulated by political groups on the Right:
"This initiative is funded by the high end; we call it
AstroTurf, it's not really a grass-roots movement.
It's AstroTurf by some of the wealthiest people in

America to keep the focus on tax cuts for the rich instead of for the great middle class."[51] Her claim was baseless – the parties began under small-time bloggers, were planned from middle class homes, cost nearly nothing for the organizers, and in many cases were unwelcoming to Republican politicians[52] – but then again, truth is relative when you're a socialist. (Exceptionally relative in Speaker Pelosi's case, having been gravely poisoned on several occasions by botulinum toxin)

The Ministry of Truth issued numerous reports about the purported right-wing conspiracy. Marc Cooper wrote in the *Los Angeles Times*, "this rash of tea parties is being organized not only by the pseudo-journalists at Fox News," but also by "a conservative lobbying outfit headed by former House Majority Leader Dick Armey."[53] Journalist Joe Conason said the Tea Parties were coordinated by a "phalanx of Republicans," and were "promoted as a new phenomenon by Fox News Channel."[54] Much as Barack Obama was once promoted as a new phenomenon by every news organization in the galaxy. And what's so bad about reporting new phenomena, anyway? Isn't that what news organizations are supposed to do?

Representative Jan Schakowsky of Illinois issued a statement that the Tea Parties were "an Obama bashing party promoted by corporate interests, as well as Republican lobbyists and politicians."[55] CNN's Susan Roesgen told viewers "this is highly promoted by the right-wing conservative network Fox." She ended her segment by saying "this is not really family viewing."[56] So, just to confirm CNN's standards: Anderson Cooper joking about "teabagging" is family viewing, but a peaceful tax protest is not.

Another common response was to slander the Tea Partiers as racists. The rallies were construed as nothing more than anti-Obama protests, which were then further construed as anti-black protests. Comedienne and NBC commentator Janeane Garofalo maligned the "racist" Tea Partiers on Keith Olbermann's primetime show:

> There is nothing more interesting than seeing a bunch of racists become confused and angry... Let's be very honest about what this is about. It's not about bashing Democrats. It's not about taxes – they have no idea what the Boston Tea Party was about, they don't know their history at all. **This is about**

hating a black man in the White House. This is racism straight up. That is nothing but a bunch of teabagging rednecks (racial slur unintended), and there is no way around that.

It's almost pathological. And again, this is about racism… These guys hate that a black guy is in the White House. These people – all white, for the most part, unless there's some people with Stockholm Syndrome…

I didn't know there were so many racists left. I didn't know that… I , I, you know 'cause as I said, the Republican hyphen the Conservative movement has now crystallized into the White Power movement… The Republican Party now depends on immigrant bashing and hating the black guy in the White House.[57]

If Garofalo had any evidence to support her claims, she forgot to mention it – not that evidence matters when it comes to accusations of racism. That's what makes racial arguments so appealing. Play the race card and the debate is dead, stalemate. The numerous Latino and black organizers of Tea

Parties probably would have had many things to say to Garofalo, but NBC did not invite them on the program. As far as NBC was concerned, they didn't exist.

President Obama chose to ignore the Tax Day Tea Parties. White House Press Secretary Robert Gibbs said the President had no specific response to the protests, but would remind Americans that he "promised significant tax relief for working families."[58] By "working" he actually meant "non-working." The "working" families are selfish, greedy, global warming inducing slobs who will soon have their wealth redistributed to people who actually deserve it.

White House officials might have appeared apathetic on the surface, but underneath the façade they were terrified by the Tea Party movement. People were hitting the streets before Barack Obama made his first tax increase. The "ignorant masses" had somehow seen the writing on the wall. What would they do when the country deteriorated into one big California?

The day before the Tax Day Tea Parties, an unclassified summary of a report by the Department of Homeland Security began circulating online. The report is titled "Rightwing Extremism: Current

Economic and Political Climate Fueling Resurgence in Radicalization and Recruitment." Its definition of "rightwing extremists" encompasses everyone who disagrees with the present administration. Veterans, pro-life advocates, Christians – all are targeted as terrorist threats. The report opens,

> The DHS/Office of Intelligence and Analysis (I&A) has no specific information that domestic rightwing terrorists are currently planning acts of violence, but rightwing extremists may be gaining new recruits by playing on their fears about several emergent issues. The economic downturn and the election of the first African American president present unique drivers for rightwing radicalization and recruitment.

Anyone resistant to federal authority is identified as a rightwing extremist:

> Rightwing extremism in the United States can be broadly divided into those groups, movements, and adherents that are primarily hate-oriented (based on hatred of particular religious, racial or ethnic groups), and those

that are mainly antigovernment, rejecting federal authority in favor of state or local authority, or rejecting government authority entirely. It may include groups and individuals that are dedicated to a single issue, such as opposition to abortion or immigration.

Veterans are described as particularly threatening:

Returning veterans possess combat skills and experience that are attractive to rightwing extremists. DHS/I&A is concerned that rightwing extremists will attempt to recruit and radicalize returning veterans in order to boost their violent capabilities.

The report mentions the Tea Party protesters in everything but name only:

Rightwing extremist chatter on the Internet continues to focus on the economy, the perceived loss of U.S. jobs in the manufacturing and construction sectors, and home foreclosures... DHS/I&A assesses this trend is likely to accelerate if the economy is perceived to worsen.

The report also warns against the radical Christian terrorists who have been wrecking havoc in the U.S. and overseas for decades (or was it some other religious group we were supposed to be worrying about?):

> Historically, domestic rightwing extremists have feared, predicted, and anticipated a cataclysmic economic collapse in the United States... Conspiracy theories involving declarations of martial law, impending civil strife or racial conflict, suspension of the U.S. Constitution, and the creation of citizen detention camps often incorporate aspects of a failed economy. Antigovernment conspiracy theories and 'end times' prophecies could motivate extremist individuals and groups to stockpile food, ammunition, and weapons. These teachings also have been linked with the radicalization of domestic extremist individuals and groups in the past, such as violent Christian Identity organizations and extremist members of the militia movement.[59]

Obama might not care about the Tea Party movement, but the federal government behind him is armed and ready to crush its detractors.

The report is egregious for two reasons. First, it suggests the fears of the "rightwing extremists" (a.k.a. average Americans) are unfounded. The idea of the government suddenly taking oppressive action in order to confront the crises is insane – or so the report implies. In reality, intelligent people have every reason to fear the government's expansion. The few times it has occurred in American history, the results have always been "cataclysmic."

The "suspension of the U.S. Constitution" and "citizen detention camps" mentioned in the report have happened before. When southern states attempted to withdraw from the union, President Lincoln replied with a lethal "No." His proposed war was terribly unpopular in the North. He had to shut down newspapers and imprison thousands of protesters to launch his tenuous attack. A year and a half later, he was losing the battle and appeared to be near surrender. For the first time since fighting began, he introduced slavery as a reason for war. He issued the Emancipation Proclamation, a statement decried by Northerners and Europeans alike because it freed no one and served only to incite violence against the women and children alone on plantations. The Confederate military won handily on the battlefield, but it could do little to stop the onslaught of attacks by Union soldiers on women, children, and elderly left at home. Entire towns were burned to the ground. Meanwhile, if a Northerner was rumored to oppose Lincoln and his Republicans, he or she was imprisoned without trial. Dissent was quashed and the South was destroyed.[60]

Most Americans look back on the Civil War and conclude the death and oppression were worth it to see slavery abolished. Regardless of one's view of the war, the era is a reminder that the government has become dictatorial before and could do so again. The Constitution was discarded by the Lincoln administration; decisions by the Supreme Court were wholly ignored. The executive branch became all-powerful. At the time, the majority of Americans believed the power grabs to be excessive and unjustified. They suffered for their expressions of dissent in prison, the grandson of Francis Scott Key being jailed at the very fort where his grandfather wrote the Star Spangled Banner.

The Lincoln administration justified its power grab by citing the crisis of the South seceding. If the present administration wanted to seize more power, it would have numerous crises from which to choose for justification. A financial meltdown, increased terrorist activity, civilian shootings, Global Warming – all could be employed to validate government growth. After a few banks failed in 2008, the government assumed the right to nationalize multiple industries. What will the government do in the face of a legitimate crisis, and at what point will dissent again become intolerable?

Second, the report is egregious because the "rightwing extremists" are not a physical threat to anyone. They have done nothing but hold peaceful demonstrations. Thousands of rallies have been held. Cumulatively, over a million people have attended the Tea Parties. There has not been a single outbreak of violence. Counter-protesters have harassed the Tea Partiers, police have moved them, and yet no unrest has resulted. The Tea Partiers have given no indication of initiating force.

The report would make better sense if it identified actual threats. Rightwing individuals have, on rare occasions, engaged in domestic terrorism (i.e. Timothy McVeigh). Leftists have a far worse track record when it comes to killing their innocent countrymen, but Obama apparently gives a pass to those types (i.e. Bill Ayers and Bernadine Dohrn). Instead, his administration hits the Right with a report that is dangerously inexact, identifying the majority of Americans as enemies of the state.

Behind the report is a concern that the Tea Partiers might just get their way. The empire envisioned by today's big-government Republicans and Democrats cannot exist without the submission of the small-government advocates. The Tea Partiers are producers. They are wealth creators. The government can grow and strengthen its power only by consuming their wealth. The Tea Parties threaten to cut off government's source of power.

The government is countering the Tea Partiers by smearing and intimidating them. Protesters are labeled as racists; dangerous, religious fanatics; deranged ex-military men; anti-abortion, anti-immigrant wackos; violent, rightwing extremists. After demonizing the protesters, the government appears justified in taking drastic action. Phone calls and e-mails are monitored more closely without court review. Reports like the one above are issued to make sure everyone knows how closely Big Brother is watching. People are frightened such that they no longer want to express their dissatisfaction in any way. The First Amendment still exists, but no one has the nerve to enjoy it.

The side with a track record for extremist violence is the side being protested. The government's smear attacks on veterans, Christians, pro-life advocates and other right-wingers is a shameful attempt to delegitimize their message and justify robbing them of their freedom. Contrary to Robert Gibbs' statements, the government is taking full notice of the Tea Parties and is attempting to thwart them with outright distortion.

Both sides are afraid. The protesters are responding with peaceful demonstrations. The government is gearing up for "extremist" opposition to their dissent.

Where is the Tea Party movement headed? It depends on the response of the Obama administration and its Pelosi-Reid Congress. If they scale back their plans, the movement will dissipate. If they continue to scoff at the Tea Partiers and persist in their imperial plans, the movement will only grow. It could end in four potential outcomes.

First, the present leadership could continue to ignore the movement and, consequently, be voted out of power in 2010 and 2012. Second, the present leadership might actually heed the requests of the Tea Partiers and, for the sake of maintaining electoral victory, revise its horrific budget (but don't count on it). Third, the Tea Parties could lead to a substantial third party movement with candidates in the 2010 and 2012 elections. Fourth, viable secessionist movements could spring up, particularly as it becomes more evident which states are prospering and which states are leeching. Texas Governor Rick Perry told a crowd at the April 15 Tea Party in Austin that Texans could and would secede if Washington failed to reform: "We've got a great union. There's absolutely no reason to dissolve it. But if Washington continues to thumb their nose at the American people, you know, who knows what might come out of that."[61]

None of the above scenarios require violence. The Tea Parties have remained peaceful protests. Independents routinely run in elections without causing any uprisings. When the United States was formed, it was understood that states could peacefully withdraw from the union if they so chose. A secessionist movement would, of course, be the most extreme outcome, and would be the most likely to draw fire from the federal government. States have tried to secede over economic issues before. The most recent to do so are remembered as racist, rightwing extremists. The federal government has made it clear any modern day dissenters will be remembered likewise.

Some Americans were horrified by Rick Perry's secession statement. Geraldo Rivera declared it treason on his Fox News show.[62] But behind the talk of secession is a sentiment shared by most Americans. They are fed up with the government intruding on their lives. Their message is simple: "Give me some space or the relationship is over."

When they talk of secession, they are not envisioning a war between the U.S. and Texas. They are merely hinting at a peaceful dissolution, after which the two republics would, ideally, have no animosity toward one another. What the secessionists really desire is an arrangement that would closely resemble the early United States: a loose alliance in which the states collaborate and trade but ultimately are free to make most decisions on their own. Their vision is identical to that of the Founding Fathers. They want the republic as it once was, as it existed when the Constitution was still followed.

The most powerful outcome of the Tea Party movement would be the formation of a political party with the sole objective of scaling back the federal government and returning power to the individual states. The party's platform would be something like this: (1) No federal income tax – each state can levy its own taxes and pay for its own affairs; (2) limited government spending, not to exceed what Washington can afford; and (3) no federal legislation on social issues. They can be left to the individual states.

Such a party would easily appeal to people on both the Right and the Left. It would be grounded in fairness, the notion that people in one state cannot tell people in another how to live. If Alabamians wanted to outlaw abortion, fine – but Californians would get to decide the matter for themselves. If people in Massachusetts wanted to recognize gay marriages, fine – but they could not force Georgians to do the same. If people in Oregon wanted to issue carbon taxes, fine – but Utahns would not have to follow suit. If New Englanders wanted to join together in socializing their health care systems, fine – but they would not be allowed to take Floridians down with them. If New Yorkers wanted to tax themselves to death, fine – but Texans would not be forced to bail them out.

Republicans perennially offer themselves as the small-government candidates. They always disappoint. A few taxes might be lowered, but the tax code is not fundamentally changed. A few departments might shrink, but outrageous spending elsewhere grows the government to new levels. At the same time, they guarantee numerous social initiatives which might look like great ideas on the surface, but imply a necessary growth of government. Compassionate Conservatism and Faith Based Initiatives set the precedent for even greater government control. And while Republicans' moral legislation might be well-intended, is it really fair for one state to dictate its values to another? Gay marriage is an incontrovertible evil in Mississippi, but in Massachusetts the culture is extremely different.

The truth is that many Americans believe it is, in fact, fair for them to impose their moral judgment on all others. Pacific Coasters are 100% certain global warming is a grave danger and they are therefore justified in wiping out entire industries in the South. Arkansans are appalled by the pagan practice of abortion and therefore are justified in establishing anti-abortion laws in Vermont.

The third party would be built for those Americans who would rather live and let live. I posit they are the majority. Their motto is: "Don't tread on me, and I won't tread on you." It isn't fair for one, culturally distinct state to legislate over another, nor for one, economically irresponsible state to leech off another. The states can still be loosely united in trade and common interests, as the Founders envisioned, but they should not be uniformly governed by a President / King / "Most Powerful Man in the World" and his one-size-fits-all agenda.

The best way to achieve a non-intrusive, small federal government is to recruit new candidates for a new party. Reform of the Grand Old Party will not suffice. The two-party system has to be scrapped. It is too tempting for each party, once it gains control, to govern as if it has absolute power. And in a sense, it does. Enough Republicans won a majority of the vote in 2000 for the party to control the White House and all of Congress. They had no check on their power. Similarly, the Democrats won a slight majority in 2008 and now control all of

Congress and the White House. They have no check on their power.

A third party would serve as the opposition whether it was Republicans or Democrats in the majority. It would make it less likely any one party would ever obtain a filibuster-proof hold on the federal government. It also would serve to bolster liberty-loving Republicans and Democrats who might otherwise be pressured by their big-government comrades. Oklahoma Senator Tom Coburn has been a champion of small government since the beginning of his political career, and yet when the bank bailout bill came to the table in 2008, he joined his Republican friends in their panicked "Yes!" vote.[63]

Most importantly, a third party would return power to Congress. The President should, in theory, play a far less significant role than Congress. If the third party could infiltrate Congress, then it wouldn't matter if an ideologue like Bush or Obama came to power. The President would always be restrained by Congress. The new party could run a presidential candidate if it wished, but that should not be the primary focus. Another Ronald Reagan will not fix the country. He might make it a better place for a while, but his reign will end and a Bush-

Clinton-Obama type will succeed him. Redefining Congress is a better solution.

The "Don't tread on me" party could easily be formed in time for the 2010 elections. Only a few congressional victories would be required to put a check on the Republicans and Democrats. The Tea Party movement could very well be its grassroots beginnings.

For now, the Tea Parties are far simpler than the government and mainstream media characterize them. The rallies are grassroots, organized by bloggers with no conclusive goal in mind. People attend the rallies for a broad variety of reasons. They would not suddenly coalesce into a rightwing militia or secessionist group. For many attendees, the Tea Parties are simply a way to vent frustrations that have been building for many years. Based on the DHS report, politicians are not the ones who need to be worried, but rather the American individuals who increasingly have their lives, liberty and pursuit of happiness threatened by an ever-growing government.

How to Tea Party

Proper Tea Party Etiquette

Tea Parties are open events. Anyone can attend regardless of their age or political affiliation. Even dogs have been known to attend (at the invitation of their masters, of course). There are no set expectations for attendees. Simply show up, have a good time, work on your tan, and make your voice heard. Attendees are encouraged to bring clever, family appropriate signs or t-shirts to broadcast their messages. Below is a collection of suggestions:

> $11 Trillion and climbing – Now that's a lot of change!
>
> "Chains" we don't believe in
>
> 3 Simple Words: WE THE PEOPLE
>
> Andrew Jackson was Right: No to Bank Nationalization
>
> April is the month when the green returns to the lawn, the trees and the IRS.
>
> Armed and Dangerous ... WITH MY VOTE
>
> Atlas will shrug
>
> Attn: Washington, No Public Money for

Private Failure

Attn: Washington, You Have Run Out of OUR Money

Bailouts + Debt = fiscal child abuse

Bailouts, Stimulus, and Pork. Oh My!

Beef Us Up - Don't Pork Us Out

Born Free, Taxed to Death

Can We Bankrupt The Country? YES WE CAN

Can We Lay Off Congress?

CAP (your income) & TRADE (your freedom)

Cap and Trade = Broke and Poor

Cap and Trade = Trap and Raid

Capitalism is NOT the problem; Ivy League politicians ARE

Chains You Can Believe In

Cut Government Spending; Fire a Politician

Cut Taxes, Not Deals

D.C. = District of Corruption

DC: Find Another Country to Pillage and Plunder

DC: If You Have Time To Read My Sign, Try Reading Some Legislation!

DC: The Longer You Stay, The Less You Remember About US

Debt is the problem; how can it be the solution too?

Do you know what happened after 1773? We Do

Don't Bail Out The Boat: FIX THE LEAK

Don't Mortgage my Child's Future

Don't Mortgage my Grandchildren's Future

Don't Mortgage the Future

Don't spread the wealth; spread my work ethic

Don't Stimulate … Liberate

Don't Tax Me Bro

Don't Tread On Me

Down With Tyranny! Up With Liberty!

DOWNSIZE D.C.

Economics for Dummies AND Congress: Spend Less Than You Earn

End The Fed

Equal OPPORTUNITY, not Equal Distribution!

Et tu, Sacramento?

FAIR TAX

Fair Tax or No Tax

Foreclose the White House

Fraud is NOT a Right!

Free Markets, Not Free Loaders

Free Our Capital Markets

Free thinkers for a free market

Freedom Works – Bailout Hurts

Get Your Hand Out of My Pocket & Leave Me Alone!

Give me liberty or give me debt!

Give us a break before WE are broken

GOD Only Requires 10%

Government is Broken

Green House Gases: Our money being burned in Washington

Help Me Mr. Obama, They Want Me To Work and Stuff!

High Taxes + Big Government = SLAVERY

HIGHER WAGES … LESS TAXES … LOWER PRICES

Home ownership is not an entitlement

Honest Change for America: The Constitution

HONK … If I'm paying your mortgage

HONK … If you don't like the word TRILLION$

HONK … If you pay my neighbor's mortgage

HONK … If You're Fed Up With Both Sides of the Aisle

HONK … If you're paying my health care

HONK … If you're paying my mortgage

HONK for Capitalism

HOPE FOR CHANGE (with pictures of pennies)

How about a 90% Tax on Congressional Salaries?

Humans First

I Am Not Your ATM

I blew my middle class tax cut on this sign

I Can Spend My $$ Better Than Government Can

I Don't Want Your Debt

I Voted for Change, Not more Taxation

I Voted for Obama, Not Debt for Our Children

I Want My Country Back!

I Want My National Sovereignty Back

I want your money (recruiting picture of Uncle Sam)

I Will Keep my Freedom, my Guns, my Money. You Keep The Change!

I would rather live under a bridge than live under socialism

I'll Pay For My House, You Pay For Yours

I'm taking back my COUNTRY: One Politician at a Time

If Dependence Is Your Idea Of HOPE, You Can Keep The CHANGE.

If Everyone Paid Taxes … We Would All Be Equal.

If You Think Health Care is Expensive Now, Wait Until it's Free

If YOU Voted Yes to Spending, Consider This Your Going Away Party

If You're Not OUTRAGED, You Aren't Paying ATTENTION!

If You're Not Outraged, You're Not Paying Taxes!

If Your Reps Vote "Tax and Spend", Kick 'em Out in 2010

Ignore Your Rights and They WILL Go Away!

Impeach Congressional Socialists!

Instead of Apologizing for America,
  Apologize TO America

Is This What You Voted For?

It's not a stimulus bill, it's a strangulation bill.

It's Your Obligation to Fix The Country

It's Time to Clean House! -- And Senate!

Join Our Cause: Restore the Republic

Just say NO to Socialism

Justice Trumps Fairness

Keep Your Bailout; I'll Keep My Freedom

Keep Your Hands Out of MY Piggybank

Keep Your Kool-Aid; I Drink Tea

Knowledge is POWER – Ignorance is
  Weakness!

Land of the FREE

Less Pork in Bills, More Pork on Grills

Let the failures fail

Let the markets work

Let US keep our money; YOU keep the
  CHANGE

Liberty is All the Stimulus We Need

Liberty: A Stimulus We CAN Afford

Limited Government Under GOD

Make Way For Liberty

Money Only Grows on ACORN Trees

More Government for The People = Less
  Freedom of The People

More Taxes = Less Jobs
My Piggy Bank is NOT Your Pork Barrel
Next Time Read the Bill
Next Time, Read the Bill Before You Sign It
No Bonus for Freddie and Fannie Executives
No More Bailouts
No Public Money for Private Failure
No Spending Without Deliberation
No Spending Without Deliberative
   Representation
No Taxation Without Deliberation
No Taxation without Representation!
No to American Socialism
No to Socialism
No USSA!
No Way, Not Today, I Can't Pay
No You Can't
O Dow, Where Art Thou
Obama - Pelosi - Reid: The Axis of Taxes
Obama: Commander and Thief
Obama has a Crisis of Competence
Obamanomics: Chains You Can Believe In
Obamanomics: Trickle up poverty
Oh ... Now I See ... Change Means Socialism
OBAMA: One Big Ass Mistake America
Our Congress is a Toxic Asset
Party Like It's 1773
Patriots Are On The March
Pay for Your OWN Mortgage

Pillage and Plunder: At Least the Vikings did it Openly

Politicians Lied and the Economy Died!

Power corrupts; Absolute Power corrupts Absolutely

Print Me a Trillion While You're At It

Proud Capitalist Pig

Proud Owner of AIG and General Motors

Push Back

R.I.P. Free Market Economy

Read My Lipstick! No More Bailouts!

Read my teleprompter: NO MORE BAILOUTS

Read the 10th Amendment - Power to the States!

READ THE BILL NEXT TIME

Redistribution just means less for everyone

Repeal the Bailout

Repeal the Legislative Pork or Your Bacon is Cooked

Repeal the Pork

Repeal the pork or your bacon is cooked

Restore the Republic, Revolt Against Socialism

Revolution is Brewing

Revolution is Brewing … At the POLLS

Revolution! Nuff said

Revolution: Part 2

Reward Responsibility, Not Irresponsibility

RIP America

S. Save; O. Our; S. Sovereignty

Save the children – Stop spending their
money

Say No To $lavery

See what happens when you give a junior
senator a credit card?

Silence IS Consent

Sleep? I'll Sleep When Conservatives Run
Congress

Socialism By Any Other Name Still Stinks

Socialism Kills

Socialism: Because Everyone Else Deserves
Some Of WHAT YOU WORKED HARD FOR

Socialism: Your Tax Dollars at Work, for
Those Who Won't.

Socialized health is NOT FREE

Solve Problems, Don't Sweep Them Under
the Table

Spare us Your CHANGE

Special Interests Get the Pork, We Get the
Beans.

Stealing Our Future

Stimulate Business Not Government

Stop Bankrupting America

Stop Giving to Charity: Just Send it to
Washington

Stop Punishing Success; Stop Rewarding
Failure

Stop Spending- Start Cutting

Stop the $$$ Presses!

STOP the Borrowing

Stop The Looting

Stop the March to Marxism!

Stop, Thief!

Tax and Spend Brings the End

TEA = Taxed Enough Already

TEA = Tyranny Elimination Army

Tea has Value, Dump the Politicians!

Tea is only the beginning

Tea Party Today: Tar and Feathers Tomorrow

The Answer is Lower Taxes. Next question?

The Answer to 2009 is 1776

The buck stops in the voting booth

The Constitution is NOT FOR SALE!

The Government is Stealing From ALL OF US

The problem with socialism is that eventually
   you run out of other people's money

The Revolution Starts HERE (with an arrow
   pointing down)

The sleeping giant is now awake

This is our pay, so we do have a say!

Trickle Up Poverty

Truth, Justice and Real Transparency in
   Washington

Two words for our elected officals: VOTING
   BOOTH

U.S. Dollar = WORTHLESS!

United States of France

USA 1776 - 2008: RIP

Wake Up America, Before Your Liberty is Gone

Wake Up America, Stop the Insanity!

Wall Street got a bailout and all I got was the bill

We ARE American Patriots

We Don't Want No Stinkin' Socialism !

We Don't Want Pork, We Want Liberty

We have had enough; Stop rewarding failure

We have to be just as vocal as the other side, or nobody's going to listen to us.

We Surround You

We the People

We The People ARE FED UP

WE The People: YOU Our Servants

We the People… Are now owned by the Chinese.

We Work Hard So You Won't Have To

Welcome to France

What part of NO don't you understand?

What's in Your Wallet. Wait a Sec… That's MY Wallet!

When Taxes Rise, Freedom Dies

Where's My Bailout?

Who is John Galt?

Who Will Bail Out The Taxpayers?

Why Should I Pay for YOUR Bad Decisions?

Yes We Can - Stop The Bailouts!

You Are Not Entitled to What I Have Earned

You Can't Borrow Prosperity

You can't multiply wealth by dividing it

You can't spend your way out of debt

Your mortgage is not my problem

Your pork broke my piggy bank

Where's The Fence?

Who is in charge? WE ARE!

Who Will be Left to Bailout the Government?

Will Work for Lower Taxes

Work Harder: The Government Needs Your
    Cash

Why Should I Pay for YOUR Bad Decisions?

YES WE CAN … HAVE EVERYTHING FOR
    FREE!

Yes We Can: Stop the Bailouts and Earmarks!

You Can't Borrow to Prosperity

You Can't Multiply Wealth by Dividing it

You Can't Spend Your Way Out of Debt

Your Mortgage is NOT My Problem

You ONLY have the Rights

You are Willing to Fight For

Your Pork Broke My Piggy Bank

Some protesters opt to display a quote:

"A wise and frugal government, which shall
leave men free to regulate their own pursuits

of industry and improvement, and shall not take from the mouth of labor the bread it has earned - this is the sum of good government." Thomas Jefferson

"All tyranny needs to gain a foothold is for people of good conscience to remain silent." Thomas Jefferson

"Every generation needs a new revolution." Thomas Jefferson

"Every government interference in the economy consists of giving an unearned benefit, extorted by force, to some men at the expense of others." Ayn Rand, *Capitalism: The Unknown Ideal*

"I am not a tool for their use. I am not a servant of their needs. I am not a bandage for their wounds. I am not a sacrifice on their altars." Ayn Rand, *Anthem*

"I refuse to accept as guilt the fact of my own existence." Ayn Rand, *Atlas Shrugged*

"I swear by my life, and my love of it, that I will never live for the sake of another man, nor ask another man to live for mine." Ayn Rand, *Atlas Shrugged*

"If you ask me to name the proudest distinction of Americans, I would choose - because it contains all the others - the fact that they were the people who created the phrase to make money. No other language or nation had ever used these words before; men had always thought of wealth as a static quantity - to be seized, begged, inherited, shared, looted or obtained as a favor. Americans were the first to understand that wealth has to be created." Ayn Rand, *Atlas Shrugged*

"Property is surely a right of mankind as real as liberty." John Adams

"Remember, democracy never lasts long. It soon wastes, exhausts, and murders itself. There is never a democracy that did not commit suicide." John Adams

"The democracy will cease to exist when you take away from those who are willing to work to give to those who are not." Thomas Jefferson

"The evil of the world is made possible by nothing but the sanction you give it." Ayn Rand, *Atlas Shrugged*

"The issue today is the same as it has always been throughout all history, whether man shall be allowed to govern himself or be ruled by a small elite." Thomas Jefferson

"Debt is the fatal disease of republics, the first thing and the mightiest to undermine governments and corrupt the people." Wendell Phillips

"Debt, n. An ingenious substitute for the chain and whip of the slavedriver." Ambrose Bierce

"It takes as much imagination to create debt as to create income." Leonard Orr

"Man is not free unless the government is limited." Ronald Reagan

"The way to crush the bourgeoisie is to grind them between the millstones of taxation and inflation." Vladmir Lenin

Again, the sign should be family appropriate and relevant to the event. The Atlanta Tea Party organizers advised their attendees: "Protest signs that are not in line with the theme of the event will be removed from the demonstration. Such signs include but are not limited to: campaigning, racially inappropriate slogans, anything that suggests violence or unlawful activity, and/or partisan slogans."[64]

The point of attending the Tea Party is to make your voice heard; however, be wary of anyone pushing a camera and microphone in your face. Numerous smear groups attended the rallies in hopes of tricking the protesters into looking foolish. Daily Kos blogger Tedshubris wrote on the eve of the Tax Day Tea Parties:

> Tomorrow, my husband and I will be venturing into the wilds disguised as a news crew to do some in person interviewers with teabaggers here in Rhode Island (if we can find any). We've got some questions lined up to ask, but I'd love to get suggestions!
>
> The great thing about owning professional video equipment is that armed with it, you

can pass yourself off as being a professional news crew pretty easily.

So tomorrow, 'WSFR' is going to send a cameraman and on air news personality out into the field to cover this 'teabagging' phenomenon.

We're going to ask open ended questions that seem to have a slight conservative bent to (hopefully) get them to open up and just start ranting. Then, we take any examples of racism, hatred, ignorance, and stupidity that we catch on camera and make a little movie out of it. Probably a YouTube special.

Here's the list we have so far

* What are you celebrating (The Boston Tea Party), and can you explain its historical relevance? [We're hoping to get some hilarious flubs from this one]

* Is this your first time teabagging? [OK, so, a juvenile one, but worth it]

* Do you approve of Michael Steele's plan to expand the GOP through a "hip-hop urban-suburban marketing strategy"? [hoping to get some juicy racist stuff from this question]

* (as an intentional misunderstanding/follow up, presuming that someone complains about wasteful government spending) 'So you disapprove of your tax dollars going to the Iraq War?' [should elicit some confusion]

Anyways, it's a start... but I'd love to have some suggestions for questions that sound fine, but should prompt an outpouring of crazy.[65]

Several protesters fell victim to the smear groups and now appear on YouTube sounding confused. The editing of the videos is far from generous and, in some instances, is utterly depraved. If a reporter singles you out for questions, ask for his credentials before giving him any material. Turn it around on him. Ask him questions. If he gets pushy or seems like he's trying to trick you, direct him to the event organizer or one of the speakers. Don't tell him off. You'd only be giving him what he wants.

How to Throw Your Own Tea Party

Anyone can throw a Tea Party. The task can be as easy or as complicated as you wish. Most rallies are initiated without the aid of any group. An individual decides he or she wants to throw a Tea Party, spreads the word in print and online, and people show up. Other organizers partner with a local political group, hold multiple meetings leading up to the rally, book speakers and bands, or purchase catering to attract participants. Those endeavors are admirable and make for an even grander Tea Party, but are not at all necessary. The Tea Partiers are fueled by their dissatisfaction with the government. Give them an outlet, and at least a few will show up.

If you would like to host a more involved event, consider forming a committee and assigning responsibilities like publicity, budgeting, community relations, entertainment, speakers, etc. The organizers of the Port Saint Lucie, Florida Tea Party held planning meetings leading up to the event, including one where participants got together and made signs. They also created an account on MeetUp.com and periodically sent e-mail updates to people committed to attending.

Speakers are a nice addition and should be relatively easy to find. Plenty of people are opinionated on politics and would be happy to give their two cents. See how your federal, state and local politicians have responded to the economic crisis. Have they consistently voted for liberty and personal responsibility, or did they jump on the big-spending bandwagon? If you're fortunate enough to have a pro-liberty politician in your midst, invite him or her to speak at your rally. Political action groups would be glad to participate in the event as well. Just be careful not to allow them to usurp the event; they might take your Tea Party in a direction you would rather it not go. When RNC Chairman Michael Steele asked to speak at the Chicago Tea Party, the organizers politely declined:

> With regards to stage time, we respectfully must inform Chairman Steele that RNC officials are welcome to participate in the rally itself, but we prefer to limit stage time to those who are not elected officials, both in

Government as well as political parties. This is an opportunity for Americans to speak, and elected officials to listen, not the other way around.[66]

If you would like to keep your Tea Party on the simple side, follow the 4 easy steps listed below. You can always expand your Tea Party later if new opportunities present themselves.

Four easy steps to throwing your own Tea Party:

1) Check to see if there is already a Tea Party planned for your area. Duplicate parties will detract from one another. Your city, town or neighborhood would be best served by one, unified event. Search the internet for "(your city) Tea Party." Check websites like Google.com, Facebook.com, ReTeaParty.com, and FreedomWorks.com. If you find that a Tea Party is already being planned, consider contacting the organizers to offer your help.

2) Build a network. Visit ReTeaParty.com and click "Start a Tea Party". They will create a website listing for your Tea Party so that others can see a rally is being planned for your area. If you use

Facebook, create an event listing and send it to all your friends. Contact likeminded family members, friends, neighbors and coworkers who might want to help you plan the party or attend.

3) Choose a location and get permission. Tea Parties have been held in a variety of locations. Government buildings are popular rally points – post offices, city halls, IRS buildings. Others have been held along major roads with a notable intersection as their epicenter. If you are expecting thousands of attendees, you might use a large public park or plaza. Try to think of places that would be familiar to the people in your area.

Once you've selected your preferred spot, contact your local government to find out if you need a permit. Call both city hall and your county commissioner. Tell them you're planning a peaceful demonstration and would like to know if you need to file any paperwork. They'll want to know the date, time, and specific location of the event, as well as the estimated attendance (give them the high end of your estimate; better to plan for more than for less). Also tell them you'd like police present at the event if possible.

4) Publicize your event. Use websites like ReTeaParty.com and Facebook.com to promote your Tea Party online. You also might create a free blog on Wordpress.com or Blogspot.com to post updates on your plans. Call local television and radio stations and offer an interview to your local newspaper. Send out a press release with your contact information. The press release should look something like this:

FOR IMMEDIATE RELEASE

Contact:
Lady Liberty
1 Liberty Island
New York, NY 10004
Phone:
Website:
E-mail:

Independence Day Tea Party in Liberty Park, New York

New York, NY – May 1, 2009 – A Tea Party will be held from 4:00 to 7:00pm on July 4 at Liberty Park in New York.

Tea Parties will be held in over 1,000 cities on July 4th. Attendees will protest the reckless economic policies of the federal government.

For more information, please contact Lady Liberty at (e-mail), or by phone at (phone number).

Updates will be posted online at (website).

# # #

Add information as you see fit. Send the press release to a reporter who covers your area. You also can submit a press release online at PR.com for free. To maximize exposure, consider releasing three different press releases: one when you make initial plans for the event; another to remind people of the upcoming date and to inform them of any new plans; and a final release just before the Tea Party.

Tea Parties:
A Photographic Sample

The following were taken at the Tax Day Tea Parties, 2009

Port Saint Lucie, Florida (photo by TheRationalActor.com)

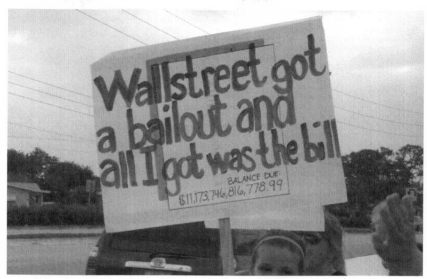

Port Saint Lucie, Florida (photo by TheRationalActor.com)

Port Saint Lucie, Florida (photo by TheRationalActor.com)

Port Saint Lucie, Florida (photo by TheRationalActor.com)

Port Saint Lucie, Florida (photo by TheRationalActor.com)

Port Saint Lucie, Florida (photo by TheRationalActor.com)

Port Saint Lucie, Florida (photo by TheRationalActor.com)

Port Saint Lucie, Florida (photo by TheRationalActor.com)

Port Saint Lucie, Florida (photo by TheRationalActor.com)

Port Saint Lucie, Florida (photo by TheRationalActor.com)

Port Saint Lucie, Florida (photo by TheRationalActor.com)

Port Saint Lucie, Florida (photo by TheRationalActor.com)

Port Saint Lucie, Florida (photo by TheRationalActor.com)

*Homeland Security at Port Saint Lucie, Florida (photo by
TheRationalActor.com)*

Port Saint Lucie, Florida (photo by TheRationalActor.com)

Port Saint Lucie, Florida (photo by TheRationalActor.com)

Port Saint Lucie, Florida (photo by TheRationalActor.com)

Port Saint Lucie, Florida (photo by TheRationalActor.com)

Port Saint Lucie, Florida (photo by TheRationalActor.com)

Port Saint Lucie, Florida (photo by TheRationalActor.com)

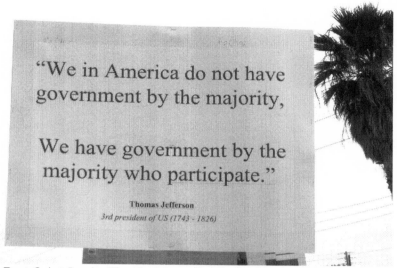

Port Saint Lucie, Florida (photo by TheRationalActor.com)

Port Saint Lucie, Florida (photo by TheRationalActor.com)

Port Saint Lucie, Florida (photo by TheRationalActor.com)

Anchorage, Alaska (photo by Jason Cline, The Fixed Pie,
thefixedpie.blogspot.com)

Anchorage, Alaska (photo by Jason Cline, The Fixed Pie,
thefixedpie.blogspot.com)

Anchorage, Alaska (photo by Jason Cline, The Fixed Pie,
thefixedpie.blogspot.com)

*Anchorage, Alaska (photo by Jason Cline, The Fixed Pie,
thefixedpie.blogspot.com)*

Tulsa, Oklahoma (photo by Susan Duncan)

"4" STEPS TO: "TYRANNY"
1 - GOV'T CREATES A "CRISIS"
2 - YOU LET GOV'T "FIX IT"
3 - GOV'T TAKES YOUR "PROPERTY"
4 - GOV'T TAKES YOUR "LIBERTY"

WHERE ARE WE NOW?

Tulsa, Oklahoma (photo by Susan Duncan)

Cincinnati, Ohio (photo by Amanda Cullen, zooinajungle.com)

Cincinnati, Ohio (photo by Amanda Cullen, zooinajungle.com)

Cincinnati, Ohio (photo by Amanda Cullen, zooinajungle.com)

Cincinnati, Ohio (photo by Amanda Cullen, zooinajungle.com)

Cincinnati, Ohio (photo by Amanda Cullen, zooinajungle.com)

Cincinnati, Ohio (photo by Amanda Cullen, zooinajungle.com)

Cincinnati, Ohio (photo by Amanda Cullen, zooinajungle.com)

Cincinnati, Ohio (photo by Amanda Cullen, zooinajungle.com)

Trussville, Alabama (photo by Scott L.)

Trussville, Alabama (photo by Scott L.)

Trussville, Alabama (photo by Scott L.)

Trussville, Alabama. "Food stamps" were handed out for food provided at the event (photo by Scott L.)

Trussville, Alabama (photo by Scott L.)

Trussville, Alabama (photo by Scott L.)

Wausau, Wisconsin (photo by Mac Bailey)

Wausau, Wisconsin (photo by Mac Bailey)

Wausau, Wisconsin (photo by Mac Bailey)

Wausau, Wisconsin (photo by Mac Bailey)

Wausau, Wisconsin (photo by Mac Bailey)

Wausau, Wisconsin (photo by Mac Bailey)

Wausau, Wisconsin (photo by Mac Bailey)

Wausau, Wisconsin (photo by Mac Bailey)

Wausau, Wisconsin (photo by Mac Bailey)

Wausau, Wisconsin (photo by Mac Bailey)

Wausau, Wisconsin (photo by Mac Bailey)

Tea Party Stats

Pajamas Media (pjtv.com) recruited hundreds of citizen journalists to cover the Tea Parties. They have some of the most comprehensive data on Tea Party attendance. The following statistics are drawn from Pajamas Media, local newspapers, and Tea Party websites.

Attendance figures are only rough estimates. Tea Party data is scarce for numerous reasons, most significantly because the majority of news outlets ignored the rallies. Even if the media had paid attention to the Tea Parties, crowd sizes are always difficult to estimate. When the mainstream media flocked to Iraq War protests during the Bush years, the stated crowd sizes were always inconsistent. Also, the Tea Party movement is purely grassroots. No overarching organization exists to track each party and collect information on its participation. If Fox News or the Republican Party really were at the helm of the Tea Parties, they ostensibly would be tallying the crowds at every party.

The list below will inevitably omit several cities, overstate attendance in some instances, and understate it in others. The figures are only meant to give an approximation as to where Tea Parties took place and how many individuals were involved.

First protest: February 16, 2009, in Seattle, Washington. Organized by blogger Liberty Belle.

Top Five Tax Day Tea Parties:
San Antonio – 16,000
Atlanta – 15,000
New York City – 12,500
Indianapolis – 12,000
Houston – 11,500

Top Five States by Attendance on Tax Day:
Texas – 92,000
California – 70,000
Florida – 55,000
Ohio – 32,000
Tennessee – 31,500

Top Five States by Number of Events on Tax Day:
California – 81
Texas – 78
Florida – 57
Pennsylvania – 35
New York – 33

A List of Tax Day Tea Parties (attendance estimates included where available):

State	City	Attendance
Alabama	Auburn	600
	Birmingham	5000
	Cullman	
	Dothan	
	Fairhope	550
	Florence	500
	Fort Payne	
	Greenville	
	Hueytown	300
	Huntsville	3000
	Mobile	1000
	Montgomery	2500
	Oleander	
	Trussville	500
	Tuscaloosa	550
	Wetumpka	420
Alaska	Anchorage	1200
	Fairbanks 1	300
	Fairbanks 2	200
	Haines	
	Homer	
	Ketchikan	120
	Kodiak	20
	Soldotna	
	Wasilla	850
Arizona	Bullhead City	
	Chloride	
	Cottonwood	

	Duncan	
	Flagstaff	300
	Gilbert	1000
	Green Valley	50
	Kingman	
	Lake Havasu City	2000
	Phoenix	5000
	Prescott	3000
	Sedona	
	Tucson	3000
	Yuma	1100
Arkansas	Bella Vista	300
	Benton	
	Caulksville	
	Conway	
	Fayetteville 1	1500
	Fayetteville 2	486
	Harrison	300
	Hope	
	Lafayette County	
	Little Rock	2500
	Mountain Home	1000
	Rogers	300
	Searcy	
	White Hall	200
California	Alturas	100
	Angels Camp	200
	Atascadero	1000
	Bakersfield	2600
	Chico	300

Chino	1000
Citrus Heights	
Danville	100
El Cajon	1000
El Segundo	1000
Escondido	3000
Eureka	1200
Fresno	5000
Glendale	500
Hesperia	
Hollister	150
Laguna Beach	655
Lancaster	
Lincoln	175
Lodi	
Los Angeles	500
Modesto	400
Monterey	600
Norco	
Oakland	
Oceanside	5000
Palm Desert	400
Palm Springs	1000
Pismo Beach	200
Pleasanton	2000
Ramona	200
Rancho Cucamonga 1	2000
Rancho Cucamonga 2	1600
Redding 1	250

Redding 2	2500
Redlands	500
Richmond	
Ridgecrest	
Riverside	400
Sacramento	10000
San Bernardino	2000
San Diego 1	5000
San Francisco	500
San Jose	1000
San Mateo	250
Santa Ana 1	3500
Santa Ana 2	2500
Santa Barbara	300
Santa Clarita	1400
Santa Cruz	60
Santa Maria	1600
Santa Monica	400
Santa Rosa	500
Seal Beach	500
Simi Valley	200
Sonora	
Temecula	2500
Thousand Oaks	
Ukiah	300
Vacaville	
Ventura	700
Victorville	200
Walnut Creek	
Yorba Linda	1000

	Yucaipa	200
Colorado	Berthoud	
	Canon City	125
	Colorado Springs	3000
	Craig	312
	Delta	
	Denver	5000
	Durango	500
	Fort Collins	1500
	Frisco	50
	Grand Junction	2783
	Loveland	1500
	Pueblo	
	Walsenburg	110
	Woodland Park	1
Connecticut	Greenwich	200
	Hartford	5000
	New Haven	2000
	New Milford	150
	Norwich	800
Delaware	Dover	300
	Georgetown	250
	Laurel	250
	Middletown	175
	Wilmington	1000
D.C.	Washington	3000
Florida	Bartow	200
	Big Pine Key	125
	Bradenton	75
	Bronson	800

Clearwater	300
Crestview	
Daytona Beach	600
Deland	1500
Eustis	1052
Fort Lauderdale	5000
Fort Myers	5000
Fort Walton Beach	650
Gainesville	1000
Inverness	
Jacksonville	2000
Lake City	
Lakeland	3000
Live Oak	850
Madison	
Marianna	150
Melbourne	1000
Naples	3000
New Port Richey	500
Niceville	100
Ocala	2500
Orange Park	300
Orlando	4000
Palm Beach	1000
Panama City	400
Pensacola	3000
Port St. Lucie	600
Punta Gorda	2000
Punta Gorda	
Saint Augustine	1000

	San Antonio	150
	Sarasota	2000
	St. Augustine	1000
	Starke	
	Stuart	2000
	Tallahassee	1500
	Tampa	500
	The Villages	1000
	Trenton	
	Venice	
	Vero Beach	3200
	Winter Springs	
Georgia	Albany	
	Athens	
	Atlanta	15000
	Augusta	3000
	Columbus	650
	Eastman	
	Gainesville	700
	Glynn County	636
	Leesburg	500
	Macon	400
	Madison	300
	Newnan	
	Peachtree City	
	Putnam County	
	Richmond Hill	80
	Rome	400
	Roswell	
	Savannah	300

	Statesboro	
	Tifton	350
	Valdosta	400
	Warner Robins	500
Hawaii	Hilo	200
	Honolulu	1800
	Kahului, Maui	250
	Kailua - Kona	100
	Kaua'i	
	Lahaina, Maui	80
	Lihue	100
Idaho	Boise	3000
	Coeur d'Alene	1000
	Council	
	Idaho Falls	400
	Pocatello	250
	Priest River	300
	Rexburg	200
	Twin Falls	250
Illinois	Bloomington	
	Champaign/Urbana	400
	Chicago	5000
	Dixon	
	Effingham	500
	Lisle	1500
	Marion	400
	Naperville	500
	Nauvoo	60
	Oswego	
	Peoria	3000

	Rockford	200
	Springfield	400
	Vandalia	
Indiana	Bloomington	750
	Elkhart	400
	Evansville	100
	Huntington	150
	Indianapolis 1	12000
	Indianapolis 2	2500
	Jasper	
	Lafayette	300
	Lawrenceburg	
	Plymouth	
	South Bend	
	Terre Haute	40
	Valparaiso	521
	Warsaw	700
	Winamac	106
Iowa	Council Bluffs	200
	Davenport	400
	Des Moines	2500
	Dubuque 1	530
	Dubuque 2	187
	Iowa City	400
	Sioux City	600
	Spencer	275
	Waterloo	425
Kansas	Fort Scott	215
	Hutchinson	2000
	Lola	

	Manhattan	450
	Marysville	70
	Olathe	50
	Overland Park	10000
	Pittsburg	
	Salina	700
	Topeka	1500
	Wichita	2000
Kentucky	Danville	200
	Elizabethtown	400
	Frankfort	300
	Louisville	1500
	Madisonville	300
	Nicholasville	400
	Owensboro	150
	Paducah	2000
	Somerset	250
Louisiana	Alexandria	1500
	Baton Rouge	2000
	Covington	500
	Hammond	
	Jennings	
	Lafayette	1000
	Lafourche	
	Lake Charles	
	Mandeville	800
	Minden	400
	Monroe	800
	Morgan City	300
	New Orleans	1200

	New Orleans	1000
	Shreveport	5000
	Slidell	500
Maine	Bangor	400
	Portland	400
	Augusta	200
Maryland	Annapolis	1500
	Baltimore	250
	Bel Air	800
	Cecil County	200
	Chestertown	
	Cumberland	300
	Frederick	1800
	Havre de Grace	350
	Salisbury	
	Westminster	300
Massachusetts	Boston	2500
	Cape Cod	650
	Lowell	
	Pittsfield	
	Springfield	400
	Worcester	1500
Michigan	Adrian	267
	Big Rapids	125
	Coldwater	350
	Farmington Hills	400
	Flushing	200
	Grand Haven	150
	Grand Rapids	3700
	Grayling	

	Grosse Point	
	Holland	300
	Houghton County	250
	Hudsonville	1000
	Jackson	250
	Kalamzoo	400
	Lansing	5000
	Lapeer	500
	Livonia Michigan	400
	Midland	500
	Monroe	
	Muskegon	200
	Plymouth Michigan	1000
	Port Huron	800
	Rives Junction	
	Saint Clair Shores	
	Sault Ste. Marie	329
	South Lyon	
	Traverse City	650
	Troy	2000
Minnesota	Austin	100
	Duluth	500
	Elbow Lake	148
	Fairmont	
	Mille County	
	Rochester	1500
	Saint Cloud	700
	Saint Paul	7500
	Twin Cities	7000
	Willmar	

Mississippi	Columbus	
	Grenada	
	Gulfport	1000
	Hattiesburg	900
	Hernando	1500
	Jackson	3500
	Laurel	700
	Meridian	100
	Picayune	100
	Tupelo	600
Missouri	Branson	700
	Camdenton	300
	Cape Girardeau	
	Harrisonville	
	Jefferson City	200
	Joplin	550
	Kansas City	7500
	Lee's Summit	400
	Ozarks	
	Poplar Bluff	250
	Saint Louis	8500
	Salem	
	Sikeston	
	Springfield	1000
	Washington	1500
Montana	Billings	500
	Bozeman	1000
	Fort Benton	60
	Glendive	165
	Great Falls	475

	Hamilton	500
	Helena	200
	Livingston	125
	Missoula	500
	Stevensville	300
	Virginia City	
Nebraska	Gering	
	Grand Island	350
	Lincoln	1000
	North Platte	400
	Omaha	150
	Papillion	200
Nevada	Carson City	3000
	Fallon	180
	Las Vegas 1	2200
	Las Vegas 2	250
	Reno	300
New Hampshire	Concord	500
	Dover	
	Keene	125
	Manchester	1000
	Plymouth	200
	Portsmouth	
New Jersey	Belmar	2000
	Flemington	750
	Hackensack	
	Jersey City	
	Morristown	3000
	Newark	200
	Piscataway	500

	Trenton	400
	Vineland	300
New Mexico	Albuquerque	7000
	Alamorgordo	80
	Aztec	
	Carlsbad	
	Clovis	500
	Farmington	1000
	Lovington	
	Las Cruces	
	Mayhill	
	Moriarty	
	Roswell	1800
	Ruidoso	200
	Santa Fe	650
	Silver City	
	Taos	60
	Truth and Consequences	
New York	Albany	3000
	Albion	
	Binghampton	30
	Buffalo	400
	Canton	1200
	Corning	1500
	Eastern Long Island	400
	Endicott	300
	Fishkill	4100
	Gardiner	290

	Gouverneur	
	Hauppague	2500
	Hicksville	
	Jamestown	120
	Kingston	
	Massapequa	3000
	Medford	
	Nanuet	100
	New York City	12500
	Norwich	
	Port Jervis	
	Riverhead	750
	Rochester	1000
	Rome	
	Sag Harbor	
	Smithtown	250
	Staten Island	500
	Syracuse	400
	Utica	
	White Plains	300
North Carolina	Asheville	1800
	Boone	350
	Charlotte	3000
	Currituck	150
	Davidson	
	Eden	
	Edenton	400
	Elizabeth City	150
	Fayetteville	400
	Franklin	
	Gastonia	100

	Goldsboro	300
	Greensboro	1500
	Greenville	275
	Hickory	700
	Hillsborough	500
	Lincolnton	300
	Mooresville	150
	Morehead City	1000
	Morganton	
	Outer Banks	
	Raleigh	1000
	Roanoke Rapids	400
	Rockingham	
	Rutherford	1000
	Southern Pines	
	Statesville	200
	Sylva	
	Waynesville	200
	Wilmington	350
	Winston-Salem	2400
North Dakota	Bismarck	400
	Dickinson	200
Ohio	Ashland	600
	Ashtabula	470
	Canton	2000
	Cincinnati	4000
	Cleveland	3000
	Columbus	7250
	Dayton	7500
	Defiance	

	Findlay	
	Fremont	110
	Lima	
	Lisbon	500
	Mansfield	1200
	Marietta	400
	Marysville	51
	Medina	
	Norwalk	200
	Perrysburg	300
	Sandusky	300
	Springfield	500
	Stubenville	
	Tiffin Heidelberg University	
	Toledo	2500
	Walbridge	
	Wauseon	
	Willoughby	75
	Zanesville	
Oklahoma	Altus	138
	Bartlesville	250
	Duncan	150
	Lawton	160
	Miami	180
	Muskogee	150
	Norman	
	Oklahoma City	6000
	Poteau	150
	Tulsa	3000

Oregon	Astoria	120
	Beaverton	800
	Bend	1500
	Coos Bay	500
	Corvallis	300
	Dalles	
	Enterprise	1500
	Eugene	1250
	Forest Grove	
	Grants Pass	1500
	Klamath Falls	
	La Grande	400
	McMinnville	
	Medford	1400
	Milton Freewater	
	Newberg	103
	Newport	
	Oregon City	500
	Portland	7000
	Reedsport	
	Rogue River	100
	Roseburg	
	Salem	4000
	Tillamook	135
Pennsylvania	Bethlehem	300
	Brookville	500
	Easton	
	Erie	450
	Greensburg	1000
	Harrisburg	2000

	Hazleton	
	Henderson	
	Hollidaysburg	500
	Honesdale	500
	Kempton	
	Kennett Square	
	Lancaster	
	Lehighton	
	Matamoras	1500
	Meadville	
	Nazareth	
	Philadelphia	200
	Phoenixville	600
	Pittsburgh	2250
	Scranton	200
	Sharon	
	South Waverly	300
	State College	
	Stroudsburg	
	Sugar Grove	200
	Towanda	
	Washington	
	Waynesburg	
	West Chester	300
	Wilkes-Barre	
Rhode Island	Providence	3000
	Warwick	
South Carolina	Charleston	
	Columbia	3000
	Florence	

	Fort Mill	162
	Georgetown	
	Greenwood	400
	Greenville	10000
	Isle of Palms	4000
	Lancaster	251
	Myrtle Beach	1000
	Pickens	
	Simpsonville	
	York	350
South Dakota	Rapid City	1500
	Sioux Falls	4000
	Spearfish	
Tennessee	Bristol	200
	Brownsville	
	Chattanooga	2000
	Cookeville	300
	Franklin	3500
	Greeneville	
	Hendersonville	3000
	Jacksboro	
	Jellico	
	Kingsport	250
	Knoxville	4000
	Lewisburg	285
	McMinnville	125
	Memphis	4000
	Monteagle	
	Mt. Juliet	1400
	Murfreesboro	2000

	Nashville	10000
	Newport	400
	Somerville	
	Springfield	300
	Tullahoma	
	Wartburg	
Texas	Abilene	350
	Allen	200
	Alpine	
	Alvin	
	Amarillo	350
	Arlington	
	Athens	400
	Austin	5500
	Baytown	600
	Beaumont	750
	Bell County	
	Belton	
	Big Spring	
	Boerne	1500
	Brownsville	600
	Bryan	
	Burleson	1500
	Caldwell	300
	Carrollton/Farmers Branch/Colleyville	750
	College Station	500
	Columbus	
	Conroe	1100
	Corpus Christi	1000

Dallas	5000
Decatur	200
Denton	2500
Eastland	
El Paso	1500
Floresville	
Fort Worth	5500
Fredricksburg	
Friendswood	600
Georgetown	1000
Gonzales	
Houston 1	11500
Houston 2	6000
Huntsville	
Hurst	300
Kerrville	500
Killeen	500
Lake Jackson	500
Livingston	
Lockhart	300
Longview	1500
Lubbock	1750
Marble Falls	400
McAllen	1000
McKinney	600
Meridian	400
Nacogdoches	2000
New Braunfels	
Odessa	500
Paris	

	Pearland	455
	Plano	
	Port Lavaca	
	Richardson	450
	Rockwall	2000
	San Angelo	
	San Antonio	16000
	San Marcos	
	Seabrook	
	Sherman	
	Southlake	1000
	Stephenville	
	Sugar Land	
	The Woodlands	7000
	Tomball	
	Tyler	1400
	Uvalde	105
	Victoria	
	Waco	3000
	Weatherford	500
	Wichita Falls	1000
Utah	Logan	
	Provo	600
	Richfield	
	Salt Lake City	2000
	Virgin	
Vermont	Montpelier	
	Rutland	300
Virginia	Abingdon	554
	Charlottesville	1500

	Franklin County	325
	Glocester	
	Harrisonburg	300
	Lynchburg	1200
	Montross	
	Peninsula	1000
	Reston	500
	Richmond	3000
	Roanoke	1600
	Staunton	
	Urbanna	
	Virginia Beach	2000
	Winchester	700
	Woodbridge	
Washington	Anacortes	
	Bellevue	1000
	Bellingham	1500
	Bremerton	
	Colfax	
	Colville	200
	Everett	200
	Grays Harbor	
	Issaquah	200
	Kennewick Richland Pasco	
	Moscow	
	Moses Lake	
	Mt. Vernon	
	Oak Harbor	180
	Okanogan	

	Olympia	5000
	Port Angeles	500
	Port Orchard	
	Pullman	
	Redmond	340
	Renton	100
	Richland	1500
	Seattle	1300
	Shelton	
	Spokane	3000
	Tacoma	
	Walla Walla	
	Wenatchee	
	Yakima	700
West Virginia	Beckley	300
	Charles Town	
	Charleston	600
	Clarksburg	300
	Martinsburg	300
	Morgantown	400
	Parkersburg	
	Wheeling	1800
Wisconsin	Appleton	3000
	Eau Claire	1000
	Fond Du Lac	
	Madison	8000
	Milwaukee	
	Wausau	2000
Wyoming	Casper	1000
	Cheyenne	880

Cody	500
Gillette	250
Jackson Hole	
Powell	150
Sheridan	

Notes

[1] Keli "Liberty Belle" Carender, "Seattleites Out There?" Redistributing Knowledge, 10 Feb. 2009, accessed 1 Apr. 2009 <http://redistributingknowledge.blogspot.com/2009/02/seattle ites-out-there.html>. For coverage of the event, see kirotv.com <http://www.kirotv.com/video/18727718/index.html>.

[2] The event was organized by Jim Pfaff of Colorado Americans for Prosperity, Jon Caldara and the Independence Institute, former Representative Tom Tancredo, and several GOP officials.

[3] Michelle Malkin, "'Yes, we care!' Porkulus protesters holler back," MichelleMalkin.com, 17 Feb. 2009, accessed 1 Apr. 2009, <http://michellemalkin.com/2009/02/17/yes-we-care-porkulus-protesters-holler-back/>.

[4] "Video: Rick Santelli's CNBC rant," ChicagoTribune.com, 23 Feb. 2009, accessed 1 Apr. 2009 <http://archives.chicagotribune.com/ 2009/feb/23/business/chi-santelli-cnbc-video>.
[5] The Rush Limbaugh Show, EIB Network, 19 Feb. 2009.

[6] "Video: Rick Santelli's CNBC rant," ChicagoTribune.com, 23 Feb. 2009, accessed 1 Apr. 2009 <http://archives.chicagotribune.com/2009/feb/23/business/chi-santelli-cnbc-video>.

[7] According to Michelle Malkin, Michael Patrick Leahy of TCOT spearheaded the events, along with Don't Go, Smart Girl Politics, Americans for Tax Reform, Heartland Institute, and American Spectator Magazine. See Michelle Malkin, "Tea Party U.S.A.: The movement grows," MichelleMalkin.com, 21 Feb. 2009, accessed 1 Apr. 2009

<http://michellemalkin.com/2009/02/21/tea-party-usa-the-movement-grows>.

[8] "About," Tax Day Tea Party, accessed 1 Apr. 2009 <http://taxdayteaparty.com/about>.

[9] Tim O'Neil, "Riverfront tea party protest blasts Obama's stimulus plan," *St. Louis Post-Dispatch* (Mo.), 28 Feb. 2009.

[10] Jeff Moore, "Stimulus spurs local protest," *The Daily Advertiser* (Lafayette, LA), 6 Mar. 2009.

[11] Sara Boyd, "Green Bay tea party rallies against federal programs," *Green Bay Press-Gazette* (WI), 8 Mar. 2009.

[12] Amber Ellis, "Thousands gather for 'Tea Party'," *Cincinnati Enquirer* (OH), 15 Mar. 2009.

[13] "About," Tax Day Tea Party, accessed 1 Apr. 2009 <http://taxdayteaparty.com/about>. The site TaxDayTeaParty.com was developed by blogger Eric Odom.

[14] Early estimates showed Tea Party attendance much lower, at 100,000 to 250,000; however, as more police and journalist reports came in, the figure quickly climbed. By Friday morning, 36 hours after the Tea Parties, PJTV had the number at 617,568 with numerous groups yet to report. Fox News estimated more than 750,000. At the printing of this book, many groups are still reporting their numbers, and the total figure could easily exceed 1 million.

[15] Matt Drudge, "FOX RATINGS SURGE ON PROTEST COVERAGE," DrudgeReport.com, 16 Apr. 2009.

[16] Glenn Beck, "Remember The Alamo — It's Time to Fight for Our Country," 16 Apr. 2009, accessed 17 Apr. 2009 <http://foxforum.blogs.foxnews.com/2009/04/16/beck_alamo>.

[17] CATO Institute, advertisement, accessed 1 Apr. 2009 <http://www.cato.org/special/stimulus09/cato_stimulus.pdf>. The economists who signed the statement against Barack Obama's stimulus bill were:
BURTON ABRAMS, Univ. of Delaware
DOUGLAS ADIE, Ohio University
LEE ADKINS, Oklahoma State University
WILLIAM ALBRECHT, Univ. of Iowa
RYAN AMACHER, Univ. of Texas at Arlington
J.J.ARIAS, Georgia College & State University
HOWARD BAETJER, JR., Towson University
CHARLES BAIRD, California State University, East Bay
STACIE BECK, Univ. of Delaware
DON BELLANTE, Univ. of South Florida
JAMES BENNETT, George Mason University
BRUCE BENSON, Florida State University
SANJAI BHAGAT, Univ. of Colorado at Boulder
MARK BILS, Univ. of Rochester
ALBERTO BISIN, New York University
WALTER BLOCK, Loyola University New Orleans
CECIL BOHANON, Ball State University
MICHELE BOLDRIN,Washington University in St. Louis
DONALD BOOTH, Chapman University
MICHAEL BORDO, Rutgers University
SAMUEL BOSTAPH, Univ. of Dallas
DONALD BOUDREAUX, George Mason University
SCOTT BRADFORD, Brigham Young University
GENEVIEVE BRIAND, Eastern Washington University
IVAN BRICK, Rutgers University
GEORGE BROWER, Moravian College

PHILLIP BRYSON, Brigham Young University
JAMES BUCHANAN, Nobel laureate
RICHARD BURDEKIN, Claremont McKenna College
RICHARD BURKHAUSER, Cornell University
EDWIN T. BURTON, Univ. of Virginia
JIM BUTKIEWICZ, Univ. of Delaware
HENRY BUTLER, Northwestern University
WILLIAM BUTOS, Trinity College
PETER CALCAGNO, College of Charleston
BRYAN CAPLAN, George Mason University
ART CARDEN, Rhodes College
JAMES CARDON, Brigham Young University
DUSTIN CHAMBERS, Salisbury University
EMILY CHAMLEE-WRIGHT, Beloit College
V.V. CHARI, Univ. of Minnesota
BARRY CHISWICK, Univ. of Illinois at Chicago
LAWRENCE CIMA, John Carroll University
J.R. CLARK, Univ. of Tennessee at Chattanooga
GIAN LUCA CLEMENTI, New York University
R.MORRIS COATS, Nicholls State University
JOHN COCHRAN, Metropolitan State College at Denver
JOHN COCHRANE, Univ. of Chicago
JOHN COGAN, Hoover Institution, Stanford University
LLOYD COHEN, George Mason University
JOHN COLEMAN, Duke University
BOYD COLLIER, Tarleton State University
ROBERT COLLINGE, Univ. of Texas at San Antonio
PETER COLWELL, Univ. of Illinois at Urbana-Champaign
MICHAEL CONNOLLY, Univ. of Miami
LEE COPPOCK, Univ. of Virginia
MARIO CRUCINI, Vanderbilt University
CHRISTOPHER CULP, Univ. of Chicago
KIRBY CUNDIFF, Northeastern State University
ANTONY DAVIES, Duquesne University

JOHN DAWSON, Appalachian State University
A. EDWARD DAY, Univ. of Texas at Dallas
CLARENCE DEITSCH, Ball State University
ALLAN DESERPA, Arizona State University
WILLIAM DEWALD, Ohio State University
ARTHUR DIAMOND, JR., Univ. of Nebraska at Omaha
JOHN DOBRA, Univ. of Nevada, Reno
JAMES DORN, Towson University
CHRISTOPHER DOUGLAS, Univ. of Michigan, Flint
FLOYD DUNCAN, Virginia Military Institute
FRANCIS EGAN, Trinity College
JOHN EGGER, Towson University
KENNETH ELZINGA, Univ. of Virginia
PAUL EVANS, Ohio State University
FRANK FALERO, California State University, Bakersfield
EUGENE FAMA, Univ. of Chicago
W. KEN FARR, Georgia College & State University
DANIEL FEENBERG, National Bureau
of Economic Research
HARTMUT FISCHER, Univ. of San Francisco
ERIC FISHER, California State Polytechnic University
FRED FOLDVARY, Santa Clara University
MURRAY FRANK, Univ. of Minnesota
PETER FRANK,Wingate University
TIMOTHY FUERST, Bowling Green State University
B. DELWORTH GARDNER, Brigham Young University
JOHN GAREN, Univ. of Kentucky
RICK GEDDES, Cornell University
AARON GELLMAN, Northwestern University
WILLIAM GERDES, Clarke College
JOSEPH GIACALONE, St. John's University
MICHAEL GIBBS, Univ. of Chicago
OTIS GILLEY, Louisiana Tech University
STEPHAN GOHMANN, Univ. of Louisville

RODOLFO GONZALEZ, San Jose State University
RICHARD GORDON, Penn State University
PETER GORDON, Univ. of Southern California
ERNIE GOSS, Creighton University
PAUL GREGORY, Univ. of Houston
EARL GRINOLS, Baylor University
DANIEL GROPPER, Auburn University
R.W. HAFER, Southern Illinois University, Edwardsville
ARTHUR HALL, Univ. of Kansas
STEVE HANKE, Johns Hopkins University
STEPHEN HAPPEL, Arizona State University
RICHARD HART, Miami University
THOMAS HAZLETT, George Mason University
FRANK HEFNER, College of Charleston
SCOTT HEIN, Texas Tech University
RONALD HEINER, George Mason University
DAVID HENDERSON, Hoover Institution,
Stanford University
ROBERT HERREN, North Dakota State University
GAILEN HITE, Columbia University
STEVEN HORWITZ, St. Lawrence University
DANIEL HOUSER, George Mason University
JOHN HOWE, Univ. of Missouri, Columbia
JEFFREY HUMMEL, San Jose State University
BRUCE HUTCHINSON, Univ. of Tennessee at Chattanooga
BRIAN JACOBSEN,Wisconsin Lutheran College
SHERRY JARRELL,Wake Forest University
JASON JOHNSTON, Univ. of Pennsylvania
BOYAN JOVANOVIC, New York University
JONATHAN KARPOFF, Univ. of Washington
BARRY KEATING, Univ. of Notre Dame
NAVEEN KHANNA, Michigan State University
NICHOLAS KIEFER, Cornell University
DANIEL KLEIN, George Mason University

PAUL KOCH, Univ. of Kansas
NARAYANA KOCHERLAKOTA, Univ. of Minnesota
MAREK KOLAR, Delta College
ROGER KOPPL, Fairleigh Dickinson University
KISHORE KULKARNI, Metropolitan
State College of Denver
DEEPAK LAL, UCLA
GEORGE LANGELETT, South Dakota State University
JAMES LARRIVIERE, Spring Hill College
ROBERT LAWSON, Auburn University
JOHN LEVENDIS, Loyola University New Orleans
DAVID LEVINE, Washington University in St. Louis
PETER LEWIN, Univ. of Texas at Dallas
W. CRIS LEWIS, Utah State University
DEAN LILLARD, Cornell University
ZHENG LIU, Emory University
ALAN LOCKARD, Binghampton University
EDWARD LOPEZ, San Jose State University
JOHN R. LOTT, Jr., Univ. of Maryland
JOHN LUNN, Hope College
GLENN MACDONALD, Washington
University in St. Louis
HENRY MANNE, George Mason University
MICHAEL MARLOW, California
Polytechnic State University
DERYL MARTIN, Tennessee Tech University
DALE MATCHECK, Northwood University
JOHN MATSUSAKA, Univ. of Southern California
THOMAS MAYOR, Univ. of Houston
DEIRDRE MCCLOSKEY, University of Illinois at Chicago
JOHN MCDERMOTT, Univ. of South Carolina
JOSEPH MCGARRITY, Univ. of Central Arkansas
ROGER MEINERS, Univ. of Texas at Arlington
ALLAN MELTZER, Carnegie Mellon University

JOHN MERRIFIELD, Univ. of Texas at San Antonio
JAMES MILLER III, George Mason University
JEFFREY MIRON, Harvard University
THOMAS MOELLER, Texas Christian University
JOHN MOORHOUSE,Wake Forest University
ANDREA MORO, Vanderbilt University
ANDREW MORRISS, Univ. of Illinois
at Urbana-Champaign
MICHAEL MUNGER, Duke University
KEVIN MURPHY, Univ. of Southern California
DAVID MUSTARD, Univ. of Georgia
RICHARD MUTH, Emory University
CHARLES NELSON, Univ. of Washington
WILLIAM NISKANEN, Cato Institute
SETH NORTON, Wheaton College
LEE OHANIAN, UCLA
LYDIA ORTEGA, San Jose State University
EVAN OSBORNE, Wright State University
RANDALL PARKER, East Carolina University
ALLEN PARKMAN, Univ. of New Mexico
DONALD PARSONS, George Washington University
SAM PELTZMAN, Univ. of Chicago
TIMOTHY PERRI, Appalachian State University
MARK PERRY, Univ. of Michigan, Flint
CHRISTOPHER PHELAN, Univ. of Minnesota
GORDON PHILLIPS, Univ. of Maryland
MICHAEL PIPPENGER, Univ. of Alaska, Fairbanks
TOMASZ PISKORSKI, Columbia University
BRENNAN PLATT, Brigham Young University
JOSEPH POMYKALA, Towson University
WILLIAM POOLE, Univ. of Delaware
BARRY POULSON, Univ. of Colorado at Boulder
BENJAMIN POWELL, Suffolk University
EDWARD PRESCOTT, Nobel laureate

GARY QUINLIVAN, Saint Vincent College
REZA RAMAZANI, Saint Michael's College
ADRIANO RAMPINI, Duke University
ERIC RASMUSEN, Indiana University
MARIO RIZZO, New York University
NANCY ROBERTS, Arizona State University
RICHARD ROLL, UCLA
ROBERT ROSSANA,Wayne State University
JAMES ROUMASSET, Univ. of Hawaii at Manoa
JOHN ROWE, Univ. of South Florida
CHARLES ROWLEY, George Mason University
JUAN RUBIO-RAMIREZ, Duke University
ROY RUFFIN, Univ. of Houston
KEVIN SALYER, Univ. of California, Davis
THOMAS SAVING, Texas A&M University
PAVEL SAVOR, Univ. of Pennsylvania
RONALD SCHMIDT, Univ. of Rochester
CARLOS SEIGLIE, Rutgers University
ALAN SHAPIRO, Univ. of Southern California
WILLIAM SHUGHART II, Univ. of Mississippi
CHARLES SKIPTON, Univ. of Tampa
JAMES SMITH,Western Carolina University
VERNON SMITH, Nobel laureate
LAWRENCE SOUTHWICK, JR., Univ. at Buffalo
DEAN STANSEL, Florida Gulf Coast University
HOUSTON STOKES, Univ. of Illinois at Chicago
BRIAN STROW,Western Kentucky University
SHIRLEY SVORNY, California State
University, Northridge
JOHN TATOM, Indiana State University
WADE THOMAS, State University
of New York at Oneonta
HENRY THOMPSON, Auburn University
ALEX TOKAREV, The King's College

EDWARD TOWER, Duke University
LEO TROY, Rutgers University
WILLIAM TRUMBULL,West Virginia University
DAVID TUERCK, Suffolk University
CHARLOTTE TWIGHT, Boise State University
KAMAL UPADHYAYA, Univ. of New Haven
CHARLES UPTON, Kent State University
T. NORMANVAN COTT, Ball State University
RICHARDVEDDER, Ohio University
RICHARDWAGNER, George Mason University
DOUGLAS M.WALKER, College of Charleston
DOUGLAS O.WALKER, Regent University
MARCWEIDENMIER, Claremont McKenna College
CHRISTOPHERWESTLEY, Jacksonville
State University
ROBERTWHAPLES,Wake Forest University
LAWRENCEWHITE, Univ. of Missouri at St. Louis
WALTERWILLIAMS, George Mason University
DOUGWILLS, Univ. of Washington Tacoma
DENNISWILSON,Western Kentucky University
GARYWOLFRAM, Hillsdale College
HUIZHONG ZHOU,Western Michigan University

[18] "Bush says sacrificed free-market principles to save economy," Breitbart, 16 Dec. 2008, accessed 12 Apr. 2009 <http://www.breitbart.com/article.php?id=081216215816.8g97 981o&show_article=1>.

[19] "Why You Should Hate the Treasury Bailout Proposal," Naked Capitalism, 21 Sep. 2008, accessed 12 Apr. 2009 <http://www.nakedcapitalism.com/2008/09/why-you-should-hate-treasury-bailout.html>.

[20] George Will, "Bailout Boundary Dispute," RealClearPolitics, 29 Mar. 2009, accessed 12 Apr. 2009 <http://www.realclearpolitics. com/articles/2009/03/bailout_boundary_dispute.html>.

[21] For further evidence of the Tea Parties' independence from the Republican Party, see, e.g., Glenn Harlan Reynolds, "Tax Day Becomes Protest Day," *The Wall Street Journal*, 14 Apr. 2009.

[22] David Hogberg, "Anti-Stimulus Protests Sprout-Up," Investors.com, 20 Feb. 2009, accessed 15 Apr. 2009 <http://www.investors.com/NewsAndAnalysis/Article.aspx?id=469322&Ntt=>.

[23] Aman Batheja, "'Tea party' planned to protest stimulus," *Fort-Worth Star Telegram* (TX), 26 Feb. 2009.

[24] Mary Lou Pickel, "Tea party at the Capitol," *The Atlanta Journal-Constitution* (GA), 28 Feb. 2009.

[25] Christian M. Wade, "Tax Protesters Converge On Federal Courthouse," *The Tampa Tribune* (FL), 28 Feb. 2009.

[26] "Group rallies against stimulus package," *The Idaho Statesman* (Boise, ID), 1 Mar. 2009.

[27] Jeff Moore, "Stimulus spurs local protest," *The Daily Advertiser* (Lafayette, LA), 6 Mar. 2009.

[28] David Servatius, "Anti-spend group throws 'tea party'," *The Desert News* (Salt Lake City, UT), 7 Mar. 2009.

[29] David Servatius, "Anti-spend group throws 'tea party'," *The Desert News* (Salt Lake City, UT), 7 Mar. 2009.

[30] Sara Boyd, "Green Bay tea party rallies against federal programs," *Green Bay Press-Gazette* (WI), 8 Mar. 2009.

[31] Tom Barnes, "HARRISBURG TEA PARTY PROTESTS 'ONGOING BAILOUT'," *Pittsburgh Post-Gazette* (PA), 8 Mar. 2009.

[32] Bill Hennessy, "Soon, there will be no one left to give," *St. Louis Post-Dispatch*, 10 Mar. 2009.

[33] Helen Eckinger, "Eola 'Tea Party' draws more than 4,000," *The Orlando Sentinel* (FL), 22 Mar. 2009.

[34] Helen Eckinger, "Eola 'Tea Party' draws more than 4,000," *The Orlando Sentinel* (FL), 22 Mar. 2009.

[35] Daniela Altimari, "REBELS WITH A CAUSE - TEA PARTY MOVEMENT VOICING ANGER ABOUT GOVERNMENT SPENDING - TAXPAYERS SOUND OFF," *The Hartford Courant* (CT), 29 Mar. 2009.

[36] "Man organizes protest in Mountain Home," *The Baxter Bulletin* (Mountain Home, AR), 2 Apr. 2009.

[37] Kevin Leininger, "Bailouts prompt local `tea party' - Organizer sick of federal spending, `loss of freedom'," *The News-Sentinel* (Fort Wayne, IN), 2 Apr. 2009.

[38] Doug Powers, "Why I tea party like it's 2099," MichelleMalkin.com, 10 Apr. 2009, accessed 12 Apr. 2009

<http://michellemalkin.com/2009/04/10/why-i-tea-party-like-its-2099>.

[39] http://janeqrepublican.wordpress.com

[40] Erika Franzi, "Countdown to Tax Day Tea Party: The view from Asheville, NC," MichelleMalkin.com, 12 Apr. 2009, accessed 12 Apr. 2009 <http://michellemalkin.com/2009/04/12/countdown-to-tax-day-tea-party-asheville-nc-organizer-erika-franzi>.

[41] Michelle Malkin, "Get ready for the anti-Tea Party sabotage and smear campaign," MichelleMalkin.com, 6 Apr. 2009, accessed 13 Apr. 2009 <http://michellemalkin.com/2009/04/06/get-ready-for-the-anti-tea-party-sabotage-and-smear-campaign>.

[42] Jim Treacher, "The past tense of 'think' is 'thought,' so the past tense of 'Tweet' must be 'Twought'," JimTreacher.com, 8 Apr. 2009, accessed 16 Apr. 2009.

[43] David B. Livingstone, "The Jibbering Teasickness of American Conservatives," North Star Writers Group, 16 Apr. 2009, accessed 16 Apr. 2009 <http://www.northstarwriters.com/dbl052.htm>.

[44] Keith Olbermann, *Countdown*, MSNBC, 15 Apr. 2009.

[45] Keith Olbermann, *Countdown*, MSNBC, 15 Apr. 2009.

[46] Rachel Maddow, *The Rachel Maddow Show*, MSNBC, 15 Apr. 2009.

[47] "Teabagging" involves a man squatting over another person's face and pushing his scrotum against the latter's mouth. CNN and MSNBC incorporated the term "teabagging" into their reports on the Tea Parties as frequently as possible, openly laughing at their sexual references.

[48] "Cable Anchors, Guests Use Tea Parties as Platform for Frat House Humor," Fox News, 16 Apr. 2009, accessed 16 Apr. 2009 <http://www.foxnews.com/politics/2009/04/16/cable-anchors-guests-use-tea-parties-platform-frat-house-humor>.

[49] Keith Olbermann, *Countdown*, MSNBC, 15 Apr. 2009. Olbermann's "teabagging" jokes included: "after all the anticipation and buildup, the teabagging exploded all across America;" they "are still considering what to do with the load; "of course it is hard to change position right in the middle of teabagging;" "if he sounds like he's got marbles in his mouth, that's just the presence of the camera" (referring to the difficult speech of an old man interviewed by Fox News); "these teabaggers claim high taxes have brought them to their knees."

[50] Ann Coulter, "Obama's recipe for change not my cup of tea," AnnCoulter.com, 15 Apr. 2009, accessed 15 Apr. 2009 <http://www.anncoulter.com/cgilocal/printer_friendly.cgi?article=308>.

[51] "House Democrat Leaders: Tea Partiers Are Racist, Nazi, Gun Nuts," The Weekly Standard Blog, 16 Apr. 2009, accessed 16 Apr. 2009 <http://www.weeklystandard.com/weblogs/TWSFP/2009/04/house_democrat_leaders_tea_par.asp>.

[52] At the Greenville, South Carolina Tea Party (attendance 10,000), Republican Congressman Gresham Barrett was actually booed by the crowd. Barrett voted in favor of the bailouts and Obama stimulus plan. He was visibly shaken by the shouting. See Adam Fogle, "Barrett booed at Greenville Tea Party," The Palmetto Scoop, 17 Apr. 2009, accessed 17 Apr. 2009 <http://www.palmettoscoop.com/2009/04/17/barrett-booed-at-greenville-tea-party>.

[53] Marc Cooper, "Anti-Obama Taxpayer Tea Parties steeped in insanity," *The Los Angeles Times*, 15 Apr. 2009.

[54] Joe Conason, "The Tea Party Brigade," RealClearPolitics.com, 16 Apr. 2009, accessed 16 Apr. 2009 <http://www.realclearpolitics.com/articles/2009/04/16/obamas_cup_of_tea_96007.html>.

[55] Eric Zimmermann, "Schakowsky: Tea parties 'despicable'," The Hill's Blog Briefing Room, 16 Apr. 2009, accessed 16 Apr. 2009 <http://briefingroom.thehill.com/2009/04/16/schakowsky-tea-parties-despicable>.

[56] "Founding Bloggers Exclusive! Our Footage Of The CNN Chicago Tea Party Throwdown," Founding Bloggers, 16 Apr. 2009, accessed 16 Apr. 2009 <http://www.foundingbloggers.com/wordpress/2009/04/founding-bloggers-exclusive-our-footage-of-the-cnn-chicago-tea-party-throwdown>.

[57] Janeane Garofalo, *Countdown with Keith Olbermann*, MSNBC, 16 Apr. 2009. Emphasis added.

[58] "PRESS BRIEFING BY PRESS SECRETARY ROBERT GIBBS," The White House, 15 Apr. 2009, accessed 16 Apr. 2009 <http://www.whitehouse.gov/the_press_office/Briefing-by-White-House-Press-Secretary-Robert-Gibbs-4-15-09>.

[59] The report is available online at http://michellemalkin.cachefly.net/michellemalkin.com/wp/wp-content/uploads/2009/04/hsa-rightwing-extremism-09-04-07.pdf

[60] I realize my history of the Civil War is unconventional. American school children are taught the Civil War was about slavery. Southerners hated blacks and wanted to keep them enslaved; Northerners loved black people as equals and wanted to free them. The end. This account is unsurprisingly gracious to the victors and woefully inaccurate. For an entirely different and well-documented account of the Civil War, as summarized in the noted paragraph, see Thomas J. DiLorenzo, *The Real Lincoln* (New York: Three Rivers Press, 2002).

[61] Kelly Shannon, "Perry fires up anti-tax crowd," *Dallas Morning News*, 15 Apr. 2009.

[62] Geraldo Rivera, *At Large with Geraldo Rivera*, Fox News, 18 Apr. 2009.

[63] Senator Coburn voted yea to the Troubled Asset Relief Program in October, 2008 (HR 1424).

[64] "Sign Suggestions," Atlanta Tea Party, 8 Apr. 2009, accessed 10 Apr. 2009 <http://www.atlantateaparty.net/2009/04/sign-suggestions.html>.

[65] Tedshubris, "Planning fun with Teabaggers!" Daily Kos, 14 Apr. 2009, accessed 14 Apr. 2009 <http://www.dailykos.com/story/2009/4/14/719961/-Planning-Fun-with-Teabaggers!>.

[66] Glenn Harlan Reynolds, "Tax Day Becomes Protest Day," *The Wall Street Journal*, 14 Apr. 2009.

4864577

Made in the USA
Lexington, KY
13 March 2010